John Maresca with Ida Manton

Ukraine: Putin's War for Russia

How the War over Ukraine Reflects Putin's Broader Effort to
Re-Establish Moscow's Control over the Whole of What Was the USSR

John Maresca
with Ida Manton

UKRAINE: PUTIN'S WAR FOR RUSSIA'S "NEAR ABROAD"

How the War over Ukraine Reflects Putin's Broader Effort
to Re-Establish Moscow's Control over the
Whole of What Was the USSR

Bibliographic information published by the Deutsche Nationalbibliothek
Die Deutsche Nationalbibliothek lists this publication in the Deutsche Nationalbibliografie; detailed bibliographic data are available on the Internet at http://dnb.d-nb.de.

Bibliografische Information der Deutschen Nationalbibliothek
Die Deutsche Nationalbibliothek verzeichnet diese Publikation in der Deutschen Nationalbibliografie; detaillierte bibliografische Daten sind im Internet über http://dnb.d-nb.de abrufbar.

Cover photos:
Heads of State or Government of CSCE participating States stand for a group photo at the Paris Summit, Palais de L'Elysee, 19 November 1990. (George Bush Presidential Library)
https://www.osce.org/event/summit_1990
Bild von Pexels auf Pixabay:
https://pixabay.com/de/photos/polizei-hubschrauber-milit%c3%a4r-krieg-1282330/

ISBN (Print): 978-3-8382-1836-6
ISBN (E-Book [PDF]): 978-3-8382-7836-0
© *ibidem*-Verlag, Hannover • Stuttgart 2024
All rights reserved.

Printed in the United States of America

The People Have the Right to Choose

"All peoples always have the right, in full freedom, to determine, when and as they wish, their internal and external political status, without external interference, and to pursue as they wish their political, economic and cultural development."

Principle Number VIII –
"Equal Rights and Self Determination of Peoples," Helsinki Final Act,
signed at the All-European and North American Summit,
Helsinki, August 1, 1975

"The space of the former Soviet Union cannot be viewed as a zone where the CSCE norms can be applied in full. This is in effect a post-imperial space, where Russia has to defend its interests by all available means, including military and economic ones. We shall firmly insist that the former republics of the USSR immediately join the new federation or confederation, and this will be discussed in no uncertain terms."

Andrei Kozyrev, Russian Foreign Minister, at a
CSCE Meeting of Foreign Ministers, Stockholm, 1992

"At Helsinki, for the first time in the postwar period, human rights and fundamental freedoms became recognized subjects of East-West discourse and negotiation. The conference put forward OUR standards of humane conduct, which have been – and still are – a beacon of hope to millions."

Henry Kissinger, "Diplomacy," Chapter 29, p. 760

Table of Contents

INTRODUCTION

When Vladimir Putin opened his brutal war on Ukraine, it was clear that his effort represented a much broader set of objectives; he intended to recover Moscow's traditional domination of all the lands which had constituted the USSR, and the Russian Empire before it. The breakup of the USSR which had taken place was really carried out for an entirely different purpose; it was intended to rid the Soviet Union of the overly-liberal Michail Gorbachev, who was simply too "Westernizing" for Russian hard-liners, in the Kremlin and in the KGB, which maintains an on-going watch over any activities which, in their view, may threaten the State.

Most of the actions which implemented the overall plan were carried out in broad daylight, with Boris Yeltsin taking a leading role. As President of the Russian Federation, the central component of the USSR, with its capital co-located in the Kremlin with the overall government of the Soviet Union, Yeltsin was able to accomplish the key to the whole plot; he "withdrew" Russia from the USSR, rendering the very concept of a "Soviet Union" with its capital in the Kremlin, invalid, and leaving Gorbachev, as President of that "Union", without an official position, or any basis for his official role.

The idea was to rid Russia of the "liberal thinking" which Gorbachev was deemed to represent, and which appeared to Kremlin hard-liners to threaten the on-going existence of the USSR — not to reduce Moscow's control over the many "Socialist Republics" that composed the Soviet Union. The change which was sought was limited to the removal of Gorbachev, and as soon as that was achieved the organizers of this action started to try to recover Moscow's traditional control over the whole of what had been the USSR, and this long effort has been carried on by Vladimir Putin, the KGB hard-liner who was designated for this role at the moment of Gorbachev's removal.

And this plan was slowly advancing, under Putin's increasingly tight control, throughout the vast regions of the former USSR ... except in Ukraine. That newly-independent state, with its long border and traditional relations with neighboring Western countries like Poland, was gradually becoming more Western-oriented, with democratic government, cross-border interaction, and a society which increasingly identified with the West. Putin has clearly seen this as a historic challenge to Moscow's control over one of the most traditional homelands of the very idea of Russia.

In this situation, it was inevitable that Putin would resort to the use of force, to prevent Ukraine from leaving the control of Russia, and he has gradually increased his destructive actions, trying to bring Ukraine back under Moscow's control.

The West—basically the countries of Western Europe and North America—has been slow to react to this threat to the very idea of the free choice of government by the people of independent countries throughout Europe. But they have gradually responded to Putin's challenge, and have joined together in support of independent Ukraine. This support must not falter, or the result will simply encourage Putin to carry out the same destruction in other countries which seek to separate themselves from Moscow's control.

This book is intended to focus the World's attention on the threat which Putin is presenting to the World—he is brazenly and openly seeking to conquer—in the old-fashioned way of military conquest—Russia's nearest neighbor, and defying the West to try to stop him. But this challenge MUST be stopped, and Putin's aggression MUST end. Otherwise we will face even greater challenges in the period ahead.

John J. Maresca—United States Ambassador, retired.

The author at the time of the Helsinki negotiations.
© John J. Maresca, 1975.

The US Delegation to Stage 1 of the CSCE, with Secretary of
State. William Rogers in the foreground to the right.
The author is shown seated, at the top of the photo.
© John J. Maresca, 1975.

Anatoly Kovalev, Head of the USSR Delegation to the CSCE,
receiving the Nobel Peace Prize on behalf of
Mikhail Gorbachev, Oslo, 1991.
© Andrei Kovalev, 1991.

The author in Vienna in 1990.
© John J. Maresca, 1990.

Presidents George H.W. Bush and Mikhail Gorbachev in 1990.
© RIA Novosti archive, image #330109.
Foto: Yuryi Abramochkin.
Licensed under CC-BY-SA 3.0
(s. https://creativecommons.org/licenses/by-sa/3.0/deed.en)

FORWARD

I was called by the press a "modern-day Talleyrand," because I was in the Talleyrand role in the contemporary equivalent of the Congress of Vienna—the "Conference on Security and Cooperation in Europe" (the "CSCE"). And I did, indeed, lead the key national delegation in the conference (the American delegation), from the time it was officially conceived in Helsinki in the summer of 1975 until its summit-level climax in Paris in November of 1990. As the de facto (and later the official) leader of the United States delegation, and the most experienced negotiator in the Western group, I led the Western participation—based on the NATO group of countries, since the European Union was still in formation—in every way except official designation.

This came naturally for me, since I had been the "Chef de Cabinet" of two Secretary Generals of NATO for five years before being assigned to the US delegation to the CSCE negotiations. In that NATO role I was as close to the leaders of the Alliance as it was possible, during the period when the Secretary General was the leader of the Western preparations for East-West negotiations. I participated in even the most sensitive discussions, as the single staff person included in the leadership-only meetings. In addition, I was outside the constraints of national delegations, as the Secretary General's key "right hand man."

I have written two books and numerous articles and book chapters, and have spoken in over sixty countries, around the world, about these negotiations and their place in history. The CSCE was very much the "Congress of Vienna" in relation to the Second World War in Europe. It helped to accelerate—and eased—the reunification of Germany, which could have been very difficult, the withdrawal of the USSR's military forces from Western Europe, the scaling-down of US and NATO forces, and the overall reduction of the American military presence on the European continent. And in the end it formed the international body which produced the "Joint Declaration of Twenty-two States," the de-facto concluding document for World War Two in Europe, which has been mistakenly overlooked by history.

But the CSCE was much more than all those things; it formed a non-threatening, all-inclusive, broadly recognized, and forward-looking bond among its participants, which gently helped the two sides of the East-West divide to overcome the differences and ri valries of the Cold War period, permitting Europe to largely recover its normal sense of itself, and of its leading place in the World. It was an essential element in the process of normalization, following the long period of division between "East" and "West" in the World's most central region.

As a half-European by birth I felt very much at home in this complex negotiating environment, and my years as the Chef de Cabinet of two NATO Secretaries General — Manlio Brosio of Italy and Joseph Luns of the Netherlands — gave me a broad, unparalleled, understanding of NATO's negotiating positions and its operational methods. I was at home in this context and had a significant personal role in the negotiating process, much of which was behind-the-scenes. I was also often invited to speak about the negotiations, and the evolving East-West confrontation, throughout the long period of this negotiation, which lasted for more than fifteen years.

Maresca served as an officer on a US Navy ship, and later became a staff officer in London, responsible for US naval communications in the Atlantic and Mediterranean regions.

This book is a personal record of that long negotiation, seen thru the eyes of an American participant, who had a central role. It touches on many of the issues dealt with in these historic East-West negotiations, and is based directly on my personal documents from that period—notes, reports, speeches, press conferences and articles intended for publication. I kept most of my personal documents, which formed the basis for this book—my speeches, notes, articles, contributions or drafts for chapters in books—and many more records from my activities during that period. I believe this book forms a unique record of a key American negotiator's view of that long negotiating process, which led directly to the official conclusion of World War Two in Europe, and the Cold War.

Comparisons have often been made between the CSCE's role during that period and the Congress of Vienna, the all-European negotiating body which formally closed the Napoleonic wars in Europe in the 19th century. Ironically, there was another Ambassador Maresca at the Congress of Vienna, as I learned when I presented my credentials at the Austrian ministry of foreign affairs in the Hofburg Palace in Vienna upon my arrival there in 1988. That previous Ambassador, Antonino Maresca, was a Neapolitan diplomat who had been serving as the Ambassador of the Kingdom of Naples to the court of the Russian Czars in St. Petersburg. European history is rich in such details, and this coincidence inspired me at the time.

I hope this personal record of that long period of negotiation will be useful and will inspire other negotiators who may face similar international challenges. Sadly, given Europe's history it seems likely that there will be more negotiations in the future which will address the same issues once again. Perhaps this book can provide some context for future negotiators who are interested in the historic evolution of Europe during the late 20th century.

This book consists of two parts. The first is my personal account of events relating to the current situation in Ukraine and hopefully a view that can inform the debate on how to negotiate a future peace agreement. Being the person who arranged the first official international recognition of the independence of all of the "newly independent states from the former USSR" — including the independence of Ukraine, officially recognized by Russia — I feel that I should share my memories and experiences from that period. At that critical moment, when we — the rest of the World — learned that the USSR had been dissolved, my first instinct was to ensure that international relations, including, above all, the relationship between "the West" and Moscow, remained stable, in order to ensure that instability would not evolve into a confrontation, leading to unintended conflict. Since, as the US Ambassador I was the leading figure in the multilateral forum — the Conference on Security and Cooperation in Europe — which was most closely focused on, and involved in, our relations with the USSR, I was well placed to set the tone of reactions to the break-up of the USSR, and to ensure that such reactions were sober and sympathetic. I felt a responsibility to show understanding, and to set a tone of assisting Russia to get through this difficult transition securely and safely, without outside interference, and without seeking advantage from what might be a delicate period of adjustment. Our responsibility was to help Moscow to stabilize its political issues, NOT to take advantage of the situation by aggressively pursuing our own interests. I felt that we, in our multi-national forum, could immediately show our understanding and friendly intentions, and that this would help the Russians by easing any concerns they might have about our intentions. By assuring stable relations with their neighbors, we would maintain calm in the region, allowing the Russians the time they needed to adjust to a dramatically different internal situation.

The second part of the book is an interview, conducted by Ida Manton, who co-authored this book. The interview took place over a longer period, and covered many aspects of the international efforts to rebuild a security structure, build confidence and mechanisms for cooperation — not an easy task in the aftermath of the Second World War.

The interview(s) were partially conducted as part of an OSCE oral history project Ida Manton has been coordinating, titled "Living Memories" and were focusing on the period that led to the signing of the Charter of Paris in November 1990.

John J. Maresca — United States Ambassador, retired.

"Ukraine! –
Putin's War and the
Broken Peace Agreement"

PART I

In the late nineteen-sixties the member states of the NATO Alliance began very private discussions about the possibility of seeking an agreed reduction of the military confrontation in Europe, and less hostile relations with the USSR and the "Warsaw Pact" – the countries of Eastern Europe which were allied with Moscow. These NATO discussions took place in highly-restricted meetings of the Ambassadors of the states which were members of NATO, under the Chairmanship of the Italian Secretary General of the Alliance, Manlio Brosio. The meetings included only the Ambassadors themselves, with Brosio permitted to bring a single assistant to ensure minimal institutional record-keeping and follow-up. As Brosio's "Chef de Cabinet" this was my role, and I was therefore present for most of NATO's preparatory discussions for the East-West negotiating process which was envisaged by the Western Allies.

When Brosio retired as Secretary General he agreed to be the single NATO envoy to go to Moscow, as the representative of the Alliance and its member states, to "explore" Soviet interest in some form of discussions, and to see if it might be possible to engage Moscow in a discussion of "mutual and balanced" reductions in the military confrontation in Europe, and possible additional agreed measures to lower the level of East-West tensions. A letter was sent to the Foreign Ministry in Moscow seeking the Russians' views on such a possibility and offering to send Brosio to Moscow for this purpose – to "explore" possibilities for East-West discussions. Brosio was thus to be NATO's "explorer" to look into possibilities for East-West discussions and, eventually, possible negotiations.

After some time had passed without any response from Moscow, a single sentence appeared in a long communique from the Soviet government, stating that the Russians "would not negotiate with a representative of a military alliance." I took this communique to Brosio, who understood immediately that this brief sentence, buried in a lengthy communique, was a rejection of the NATO offer to have him open discussions with Moscow. That possibility was then immediately dropped, and Brosio retired to his home in Torino, where he was elected to the Italian Senate.

But at the same time the Russians approached the government of Finland, very privately, pressuring them to issue invitations to all the countries of Europe and North America to join in general discussions of possibilities for reducing the military confrontation in Europe. Moscow clearly believed that a broad discussion including many individual national representatives would be a more advantageous format, permitting the Russians to divide the Western allies and opening divisions among them. This unstructured discussion began at a conference hall near Helsinki called "Dipoli," and the meetings which followed took that name. These "Dipoli" negotiations eventually produced a lengthy and detailed agenda for a massive conference which was to follow, engaging all the governments of Europe and North America in a broad negotiation, to take place in Geneva, with the concluding Summit-level session to be, once again, in Helsinki. The one European country that went missing—because it did not respond to the Finnish invitation—was Albania, which joined the resulting conference some years later.

These preparatory discussions in Helsinki produced a lengthy and detailed agenda and procedural rules for a multifacetted East-West negotiation covering three "baskets" of issues: international security and basic principles of relations among states, economic and environmental issues, and cultural and informational exchanges among states. This agenda-plus-rules was approved and signed at a summit-level signing ceremony in Helsinki in 1973. The substantive negotiations which followed took place in Geneva, and lasted for two years.

I was recruited by George Vest, the designated Ambassador to lead the US delegation in this broad negotiation, to be his deputy, and when Vest was abruptly transferred to Washington only days before the opening of negotiations in Geneva, I pursued the negotiations until their conclusion, as the Deputy Head of the US Delegation. As a former Naval Officer, on the staff of the Admiral who was the Commander in Chief of all US Naval Forces in the Eastern Atlantic and the Mediterranean, I had useful military experience, and I was the only person in the US delegation who had been present during the preparatory consultations at NATO, so I understood the "game plan" of the Western Allies, and played a major role in guiding the American participation in the negotiations leading to the first CSCE summit, in Helsinki in 1975.

Maresca in the Sahara Desert, while he was assigned as the Officer-in-Charge of a US Naval communications station in that region, during his US military service in Morocco.

Years later, during the subsequent CSCE negotiating session, as we prepared for another summit-level meeting, convened jointly by Francois Mitterrand and Mikhail Gorbachev, I was the Ambassador and Head of the US Delegation, as we concluded the long CSCE negotiating process and produced the agreement formally closing the Cold War with an All-European Summit meeting in Paris on November 20, 1990. That agreement was optimistically called the "Charter of Paris for a New Europe," and marked a turning-point in the evolution of East-West relations.

I was thus the American diplomat who was most closely involved in the long, multilateral effort to reach a peaceful, universally-agreed settlement in Europe, including the USSR, as the Cold War wound down at the end of the twentieth century. In the process I negotiated, as the US representative, the only peace agreement concluding World War Two in Europe — the "Joint Declaration of Twenty-two States," which was negotiated privately among the representatives of the states which were participants in that war, "on the fringes" of the full CSCE negotiations in Vienna. The "Joint Declaration" was signed the day before the full CSCE summit meeting in Paris in 1990, when the landmark "Charter of Paris for a New Europe" was formally signed by the Heads of State or Government of all the countries of Europe and North America. These are the formal agreements which the Russian President Vladimir Putin has deliberately broken with his brutal war on Ukraine.

When the USSR was dissolved in 1991, I was sent by Secretary of State James Baker as a special Ambassadorial envoy to open direct American diplomatic relations with each of the "Newly Independent States from the former USSR." This was Baker's recognition of my key role in the negotiations which had preceded the break-up of the USSR. My mission at that time was to visit each of these new states with a special delegation, to convey America's interest in having friendly and positive diplomatic relations with them, and to announce that we would soon open an official embassy in their capital. The first new capital city which I visited on that heavily symbolic mission was Kiev.

Maresca on board his specially assigned US Air Force executive jet, on his mission to symbolically open direct US diplomatic relations with the "Newly Independent States from the Former USSR", with his staff presenting him with a surprise birthday cake, as the plane crosses Siberia.

During my diplomatic career I lectured and spoke on issues related to these events, and on international relations in general, in more than 60 countries—on every continent except Australia. And I have written several books and numerous articles and book chapters on the historic sequence of overlapping negotiations which I carried out on behalf of the USA, including the complex "Helsinki" negotiating process, which began in 1973 and closed the post-World War Two period in Europe in 1991. This new book, which focusses on the place of Ukraine within the international situation in Europe during this period, is a personal summary of my experience during that long period of negotiation and historic evolution, as well as the issues we faced, viewed with the full advantages of retrospect and the passage of time. This book recalls the evolution of the situation of Ukraine, and Putin's aggression against it. It recalls Russia's solemn undertaking in 1975 that none of their weapons "will ever be used except in self-defense or otherwise in accordance with the Charter of the United Nations,"[1] and that Russia will "refrain from the threat or use of force against the territorial integrity or political independence of any State, from seeking to change existing borders by threat or use of force".[2]

These commitments were solemnly undertaken by all the States of Europe and North America, including Russia, on 19 November, 1990, and Putin, like the Russian state, is bound by them. Given his deliberate, and spectacular, flaunting of these obligations, he must go—he does not merit the recognition of the Russian people, nor of the international community.

This book recounts how we got to the situation we are in, how Ukraine became the subject of Putin's reckless aggression, and why the international commitments that Russia has undertaken—to respect peaceful international relations, and the established, recognized national borders in Europe—are being grossly ignored and violated.

When Vladimir Putin opened his brutal war on Ukraine, it was clear that his effort represented a much broader set of objectives; he intended to recover Moscow's traditional domination of all the lands which had constituted the USSR, and the Russian Empire before it. The breakup of the USSR which had taken place was really carried out for an entirely different purpose; it was intended to rid the Soviet Union of the overly-liberal Michail Gorbachev, who was simply too "Westernizing" for Russian hard-liners, in the Kremlin and in the KGB, which maintains an on-going watch over any activities which, in their view, may threaten the State.

Most of the actions which implemented the overall plan were carried out in broad daylight, with Boris Yeltsin taking a leading role. As President of the Russian Federation, the central component of the USSR, with its capital co-located in the Kremlin with the overall government of Soviet Union, Yeltsin was able to ac-

---

1   Joint Declaration of Twenty-two States, signed on 19 November 1990 in Paris. See the full text in Annex 1
2   Ibid.

complish the key to the whole plot; he "withdrew" Russia from the USSR, rendering the very concept of a "Soviet Union" with its capital in the Kremlin, invalid, and leaving Gorbachev, as President of that "Union", without an official position, or any basis for his official role.

But the idea was to rid Russia of the "liberal thinking" which Gorbachev was deemed to represent, and which appeared to Kremlin heard-liners to threaten the on-going existence of the USSR — not to reduce Moscow's control over the many "Socialist Republics" that composed the Soviet Union. The change which was sought was limited to the removal of Gorbachev, and as soon as that was achieved the organizers of this action started to try to recover Moscow's traditional control over the whole of what had been the USSR, and this long effort has been carried on by Vladimir Putin, the KGB hard-liner who was designated for this role at the moment of Gorbachev's removal.

And this plan was slowly advancing, under Putin's increasingly tight control, throughout the vast regions of the former USSR ... except in Ukraine. That newly-independent state, with its long border and traditional relations with neighboring Western countries like Poland, gradually became more Western-oriented, with democratic government, cross-border interaction, and a society which increasingly identified with the West. Putin clearly has seen this as a historic challenge to Moscow's control over one of the most traditional homelands of the very idea of Russia.

In this situation, it was inevitable that Putin would resort to the use of force, to prevent Ukraine from leaving the control of Russia, and he has gradually increased his destructive actions, trying to bring Ukraine back under Moscow's control.

The West, including the countries of Western Europe and North America, have been slow to react to this challenge to the very idea of the free choice of government by the people of independent countries throughout Europe. But they have gradually responded to Putin's challenge, and have joined together in support of independent Ukraine. This support must not falter, or it will simply encourage Putin to carry out the same destruction in other countries which seek to separate themselves from Moscow's control.

Opening East-West Negotiations in Europe

In the late 1960's NATO began to prepare for some form of negotiations with the USSR, seeking to lower the military confrontation
in Europe and the level of weapons waiting there for a possible
East-West war. As a way to initiate some form of negotiation the
NATO Allies proposed to send its out-going Secretary General to
Moscow to "explore" possibilities for some initial discussions.
Brosio awaited a response from Moscow for some time, with basic
plans for a visit to Moscow, accompanied by one person—his Chef
de Cabinet, a US career diplomat and former naval officer—
myself. But the Brosio Mission never took place—a brief sentence
in a lengthy and very general communique from Moscow said
that the Russians "would not negotiate with a representative of a
military alliance."

The Conference on Security and Cooperation in Europe—
CSCE, was perhaps the broadest East-West watershed since the
Second World War. A wide-ranging, multifaceted negotiation, the
CSCE culminated, in a 35-nation summit in Helsinki July 31-
August 1, 1975, which has been compared with the Congress of
Vienna and the 1919 Peace Conference in Versailles. At Helsinki
an unprecedented assembly of national leaders signed the "Final
Act" of the CSCE, a 30.000 word document which serves many
functions, some tacit and some explicit.

It is a surrogate for a World War II Peace Treaty. It sets
guidelines for interstate behavior, and an implicit framework for a
continuing system of East-West contacts. It establishes a relationship between all the European countries and the East-West equation, and brings together the many fields available for East-West
negotiations. Like an essay, history has its punctuation points as

well as its nouns and verbs, and Helsinki provided such a point in the postwar evolution of Europe.[3]

Following the failure of NATO's attempt to open a negotiating process with its former Secretary General as its single representative, the government of Finland, prompted secretly by Moscow, invited all the countries of Europe and North America — big and small — to participate in informal discussions, without a prepared agenda, to take place at a conference center called "Dipoli," near Helsinki. These open-ended discussions convened on November 22, 1972, and evolved into what were called "Multilateral Preparatory Talks (MPT)" to produce a detailed agenda covering three "baskets" of related subjects, as well as basic rules of procedure to organize the negotiations which were to follow. The agenda covered the broad range of issues among the countries of Europe at that time — political and security issues, basic principles of interstate relations, economic and cultural matters, and the Western concept of "freer movement of people and ideas" among the states of Europe and North America. In view of my earlier role, I was recruited and assigned to join the American delegation, led by a Senior Foreign Service Officer, George Vest, during the discussions at Dipoli, and I continued as the Deputy US negotiator, and later as the Ambassador and Head of the US Delegation, through two summit-level signing ceremonies — the opening meeting in Helsinki and the final signature, in Paris, on November 20, 1990, of what was named "The Charter of Paris for a New Europe." I was thus the American who was most closely associated with this vast international negotiating process from its beginnings in NATO's preparatory discussions, to the formal opening in Helsinki in 1972, and until the final signature session in Paris in 1990.

These negotiations, which were intended to conclude the Cold War that had dominated international relations among the States of Europe and North America since the end of World War Two, were held from 1972-1990 — in Helsinki, Geneva and Vienna, punctuated by a first summit meeting in Helsinki in 1975, and

---

[3]   Helsinki, by John Maresca, 1986

concluding with an all-European and North American summit gathering in Paris in 1990, formally closing World War Two in Europe, as well as significantly reducing the East-West confrontation which had dominated the European situation since the end of the Second World War, and was referred to as the "Cold War." These developments were accelerated by the popular unrest in Germany, which led to full German reunification and the general withdrawal of Russian forces from Eastern Germany. The peaceful evolution of these dramatic developments was facilitated on the Soviet side by the leader of the USSR, Mikhail Gorbachev, without whom they might not have evolved as they did.

But conservatives within the USSR saw these developments as detrimental to the interests of the Soviet State, and sought remedies which were designed to maintain the USSR's leadership role in the East. They set about to take steps which would ensure the continuation of Moscow's leadership, especially its long-standing control of the whole of the USSR, and would remove Mikhail Gorbachev — considered too liberal and Western-leaning — from his leadership role. This was accomplished by withdrawing Russia from the Soviet Union, thus effectively eliminating the "Soviet Union" as a sovereign entity, and making each of the multiple republics which comprised the USSR into sovereign, independent countries, for the first time in their history. By eliminating the entity known as the "Soviet Union," this maneuver effectively left Gorbachev without any official position and sidelined him as a political leader in Moscow. This was a very important turning point in the East-West relations in the post-WWII period.

In the early days in Helsinki relations were very distant, especially between the two opposing blocs, NATO and the Warsaw Pact. Each had very different, very rigid views, subject to group agreements among all the member states in their bloc. When we were preparing for the CSCE summit in Paris, the situation was quite different. The leader of the Soviet Union was Mikhail Gorbachev, who was a very rational person and I think was genuinely looking for ways to create a more positive relationship with the West. He found a like-minded person in the French president

Francois Mitterrand. Mitterrand was a socialist who was actively looking for ways to build closer relations with the Soviet Union.

At that time, I was the senior expert on France in the State Department as the director of relations with Western Europe. Many Americans—business leaders and other prominent persons—came to see me to ask for my analysis of how Europe was evolving. They were concerned that France under Mitterrand, who had included French communists in his government, was getting too close to the Russians. But I knew France pretty well, and I knew Mitterrand personally, and I understood his game. He was playing French politics, to ensure the support of French communist voters, while avoiding any real concessions to the communist party.

Getting Gorbachev to Paris was a double win, politically, for Mitterrand, and gave him a leadership role among the whole European group. But it doomed Gorbachev. Moscow hardliners viewed him as too "Westernizing," and soon we saw Boris Yeltsin withdraw Russia from the Soviet Union in order to eliminate Gorbachev, who was left without any meaningful position. And at the same time Yeltsin introduced Putin as his successor. Russia's future course was fixed: Putin, with his crucial ties to the KGB, was mandated to re-assemble Russia's dominance over the whole of what had been the Soviet Union—his life-long mission. And that is what has been playing out, before our eyes, all these years: the attempted, KGB-assisted, re-establishment of Moscow's full control over the whole of what was the Soviet Union. With just one hold-out, but an important one: Ukraine.

Negotiations towards confidence building, lessening military confrontation and promoting disarmament

On 9th March 1989 President Bush announced the beginning of a process of great importance for the people of Europe, the United States, Canada, and for all who share the hope of a safer and more secure Europe. It was a process planned to take place in Vienna, where the CSCE, NATO and the Warsaw Pact countries started two negotiations whose goal was to reduce the threat of conventional weapons in Europe: one on Conventional Armed Forces in Europe (CFE) and another separate negotiation on further Confidence-and Security-Building Measures (CSBMs).

The CSBM negotiations were to address the problem of mistrust in the military and security spheres and the risk of confrontation arising from miscalculation. The US went into these negotiations with an aim to lift the veil of secrecy from certain military activities and forces and thus contribute to a more stable Europe. Unlike traditional arms control negotiations that were looking at ways to reduce the weapons of war, CSBMs did not entail limitations on force capabilities or structure. Instead, they were measures built to reduce the likelihood that these weapons will ever be used. CSBMs were designed to reduce mistrust and misunderstanding about military capabilities and intentions by increasing openness and predictability in the military environment.

> "We and our NATO allies share a common commitment to democratic values, respect for each other's sovereignty, and support for a strong defense. NATO's approach to these negotiations, therefore, rests on two important principles: that maintaining strong and modern defenses is essential to our security and freedom; and that negotiated and effectively verifiable agreements can enhance our security and the prospects for lasting peace".[4]

These negotiations were seen as part of a larger process, one which was intended to address both the causes and the symptoms of the post-WWII-divisions in Europe. The underlying thinking behind crafting these discussions was that progress in the military field alone was assessed not to be enough to bring enduring peace. "What is needed is genuine reconciliation and an end to the division of Europe. True security cannot exist without guarantee of human rights and basic freedoms for all people", stated President Bush on the outset of this intricate negotiation process, in which I had one of the key roles.

---

[4]   Statement by President Bush in: "Strengthening Stability Through Openness", Publication of the United States Department of State, Bureau of Public Affairs, Editor: Sharon R Haynes. April 1989.

I was, in fact, a long-time negotiator on what are called "arms control" issues (professionals did not like to talk in terms of "arms reduction" or "disarmament" so we use terms like "arms control"). It was one of our first successful negotiations on such matters with the Russians — and the State Department publication "Strengthening Stability Through Openness" even shows photos of our "no notice" arms control inspections, as agreed in the CSCE arms control negotiations, which were a break-thru — an agreed innovation at that time, and very difficult to get the Russians to agree to! I had been the Assistant Secretary of Defense, in the Pentagon, responsible for defense issues in Europe, immediately before taking up this Ambassadorial assignment, so I was very familiar with the military situation in the European region.

One has to remember that this was the period when one of our officers, on a routine inspection of the "line of separation" in Berlin, was shot by a Russian border control guard in Berlin, and bled to death because the Russian guards would not permit his sergeant to give him elementary first aid — they fired shots directly at him every time he tried to do something! All the occupying powers ran routine rounds of inspection, with a military officer and his driver, doing the circuit around occupied Berlin. It happened three times a day, every day. On one of those days, a Russian soldier — out of the blue — shot our officer! The incident almost resulted in a military retaliation, which literally could have started World War Three! I was the Assistant Secretary of Defense responsible for Europe at that time, and I can confirm that — in the Pentagon — we were ready to retaliate militarily against those Russian units in Berlin, which could easily have plunged us into a new World War. In the Pentagon there was a strong majority in favor of a "meaningful retaliation!" — the Russians had killed one of our officers, on a routine inspection tour which was carried out twice a day — by both the Russians and us! Instead, we chose (on the basis of my proposal) to negotiate on measures which were meant to ensure safety — especially by armed patrols. That is where those negotiations came from, and why I was chosen to be the negotiator — I had been an Assistant Secretary of Defense. I was thought to understand the military view of such matters, and

I actually did bring together all the Chiefs of Staff of all the military forces of all the members of NATO and the Warsaw Pact, and hosted them all, along with my friend General Colin Powell, our Chief of staff[5]. I became a close colleague of Colin Powell when I was in my position in the Pentagon. At the start of that period, he was a military aid to the Secretary of Defense, so I often saw him because I also worked for the Secretary of Defense, who was Cap Weinberger at that time. I then went to Vienna as a negotiating Ambassador, and Colin became the Chairman of the Joint Chiefs of Staff. He was, incidentally, the first black person in that position, and became a world-wide celebrity. I then got him to come to Vienna, on the basis of (my idea) of having a meeting in the CSCE context among the Chiefs of Staff of all the member states of the CSCE! And they all came, in their military uniforms, with Colin Powell as the absolute star!

So, much later, when I became the negotiator on "Military Confidence Building Measures" I proposed a discussion of that incident, to find ways to avoid such incidents. It was approved, and that became the centerpiece for the meeting of all the Chiefs of Staff of the states which participate in the CSCE! It was an incredible sight — all those senior Generals in their uniforms — it really attracted the press. It was a photographer's absolute dream! And I arranged for all those generals to come to my residence for lunch with my friend, Colin Powell! His assistant on that trip was none other than Condoleezza Rice, who was in her first job in Washington, as the Pentagon's top expert on the Russian Armed Forces. So, my entourage consisted of General Colin Powell and Condoleezza Rice. As part of the visit, Colin Powell actually had a useful private discussion, over lunch at my residence, with his Soviet opposite number. That was the only time there has been such direct, personal contact between the two men in those two positions. And Powell was great in that role — such a likable and friendly person — totally disarming. That was why I concocted that meeting — I knew he would be a star in such a role! I then gave a big luncheon

---

5   In the US system the officer in that role is called the "Chairman of the Joint Chiefs of Staff".

for him with all the other Warsaw Pact Chiefs of Staff—just them—with short personal and private meetings with each one of them. That was a moment to remember—they unloaded in private with Powell, who was very "sympathique" personally, and no one could doubt his sincerity.

Colin moved on to the White House and although he wanted to take me to the White House, I was sent as Ambassador to the negotiations in Vienna instead—to continue negotiating with the Russians.

In Vienna we sought to build upon and expand the Stockholm measures in order to further the process of confidence-and security building, based on mutual respect, cooperation between East and West, and a common interest in security and stability. There were opportunities we felt we must pursue, but there were realities we could not ignore. The cold war was not a mirage. It was a real international situation with identifiable characteristics: the political division of Europe, the militarization of East-West relations, and the competition between two largely incompatible social and economic systems.

What became obvious to me at the time was that nations cannot be expected to reduce their military forces unless they have some measure of confidence that their neighbors harbor no hostile intentions toward them. Massive Warsaw Pact deployments of offensively oriented forces throughout Central Europe did not inspire confidence. In addition to the closed frontiers, suppression of political and labor movements, and the secrecy which has shrouded virtually all aspects of Warsaw Pact military affairs, and it was no wonder that the West had viewed its neighbors to the East with suspicion and fear.

Another important realization was that the security of nations can neither be fully measured nor ultimately achieved through military means alone. Indeed, the military confrontation which has plagued Europe for a long time was the reflection-not the cause-of the political and social division of the continent. I believed back in those days that true and lasting security for all the nations and peoples of Europe can only be built upon a foundation of confidence: confidence of nations in their neighbors and confidence of citizens in their governments.

Our efforts were only part of a broader process. The confidence and openness we were looking for in military affairs had to also extend to the relationship between governments and the governed throughout Europe. Only when ideas, people, and infor mation move freely across borders, and individuals everywhere have a say in the decisions which affect their lives, will we be able to achieve a Europe which is truly stable and secure. The negotiations we were undertaking in Vienna were an important part of this larger picture. They were aimed at increasing stability and security in Europe through greater openness and mutual understanding in the military field. Success in this endeavor could only be measured in terms of improved security for all 35 states represented here. We knew and stood firm on the position not to enter into any agreement in this negotiation which would erode the West's capacity to defend itself. We were willing, though, to explore all possibilities and consider all proposals as a part of our continuing task of contributing to the stability and security of Europe. We called upon all 35 CSCE participating states to contribute to this objective, which we saw as a matter of prudence, not naiveté. Our sincere hope was that those negotiations will contribute to the security, and ultimately to the freedom, of all Europeans. And we went a long way in building the architecture for continued dialogue, arms control and lessening of military confrontation.

Dissolution of the USSR and the "Newly Independent States"

On December 25, 1991 it was announced in Moscow that the USSR had been officially dissolved, and that the states which had comprised that "union" were now fully independent states. This included the independent states of Russia—the "Russian Federation"—and Ukraine, both of which had existed as individual member states within the "Union" of "Soviet Socialist Republics" throughout the history of the USSR. This totally un-anticipated dismantling of the USSR stunned the world, which took some time to understand all of its implications—historical, political and practical—and to respond in appropriate ways. The dissolution of the USSR side-lined Gorbachev—its President—who was left with no official position, and placed the President of the Russian Federation—Boris Yeltsin—in a central role as the leader of the government of the strongest, and most central, Republic, conveniently occupying the Kremlin and effectively in control of the State. Outside of Moscow, each one of the "Soviet Republics" which had formed the USSR gingerly and carefully began to act as an independent country.

When, that morning, I arrived at my office, in Prague, where I was attending a CSCE meeting, it was still very early because I was always the first to arrive. Reading the overnight telegrams I learned that the USSR had been dissolved, and that the Russian national flag had been hoisted, at midnight, over the Kremlin. So, I started to think what I should do right away, on that day.

It was still early morning, European time. Washington would still be sleeping for another four or five hours. That gave me some time to sort things out. The first thing I did was to assemble my staff—about four people who were there with me for the next session of the main body of the CSCE, which was going to meet that afternoon. I asked them to find out if there were representatives of what immediately became known as "the Newly-Independent States from the Former USSR" present in Prague—where the full membership of the CSCE was scheduled to meet that afternoon. I figured that we needed to organize the situation before that meeting. My colleagues then worked with the Czech telephone operators in our conference center, and began to identify the representatives of what immediately became known as the "Newly-independent States from the former USSR."

It took some time, but we started to learn that—to our surprise—there were, indeed, identified representatives of each of the Newly-independent States, right there in the city! I have never been completely sure how that was the case—my guess is that these people, who were all sorts of businessmen, etc.—were known to the Czech authorities as informal representatives of their regions of the USSR, and that they simply assumed that role in that situation.

So my staff contacted each one of these representatives and invited them to come for a brief meeting with me, before the full CSCE meeting that afternoon. Contacts were made, with the help of our Czech contacts, and each of these (informal) representatives came to my office for an informal discussion.

Each one of those new diplomats—all businessmen who had normal, private business in Prague—came to my office as invited, and I greeted each of them as the new, de facto, local representative of one of the "Newly Independent States from the Former USSR." I explained to each of these representatives that, in my view—and surely the view of the other member-states of the CSCE—their newly-independent state was already a fully-legitimate member of the CSCE, since it had already been a member while their country was a part of the USSR, which was a full member. So I maintained that they were entitled to be seated immediately in the CSCE as newly-independent states from the former USSR. I informed them that I would be arguing this position with the other members of the CSCE, and would take this position at the meeting of the full CSCE, which was scheduled to take place that very afternoon. I suggested that each of these de facto representatives of one of the newly-independent states from the former USSR should be available to represent his country at that moment.

All of these representatives said they would check with their governments, and would be available—and prepared—that very afternoon—to represent their newly-independent country in the CSCE if called upon to do that.

I convened an urgent meeting of the western countries in the CSCE, and explained what I planned to do: to immediately accept these "newly independent" states as full members of the CSCE, on the logical grounds that they ALREADY WERE members of the CSCE, as parts of the USSR—one of the founding states of the CSCE. I also explained this logic, and my intentions, to the other state representatives who were planning to participate in the meeting that afternoon, as well as the conference secretariat, who I asked to be prepared to implement this scenario.

When the meeting of the CSCE convened that afternoon, as was previously scheduled, I immediately took the floor and explained the logic of the situation, as I saw it: the Newly Independent States from the former USSR were all, already, de facto members of the CSCE, since their countries had been integral parts of the CSCE as parts of the sovereign state of the USSR, which was one of the founding members of the CSCE. These new countries were, therefor, entitled to full membership of the CSCE, along with the state of Russia, which was the de facto successor state to the USSR.

The full membership of the CSCE agreed with this logic, and a few national members took the floor to confirm this. The chairman asked if there was any disagreement with this position, and there was none—not a single representative objected to it. The chairman then asked if there was unanimous agreement that these new states should be immediately seated as full members of the CSCE, and there was no objection, so this was also agreed.

The Chairman announced a brief recess while the secretariat added the place-cards for each of the new state members to the alphabetical placement of delegations around the large, round conference table at which we were all seated. The previous membership then again took their places, and the Chairman asked the secretariat to invite the representatives of the new member states to take their seats at the conference table. Each new representative then entered the huge conference hall, and found his way to his new country's place at the table, in the normal alphabetical order by the names of the member states. It was a dramatic moment

When all the new state representatives had found their places at the huge round table, and were seated, there was a long and enthusiastic round of applause: the CSCE had managed what could have been a challenging situation, and had emerged as a—somewhat adjusted—assembly, with new members and a new history. It was a truly historic moment, which held many implications for the on-going history of Europe.

This historical significance is now, ironically, displayed very sharply by Putin himself, in his bloody war on Ukraine. The Ukrainians are dying in great numbers to retain, and maintain, the independence which they unexpectedly obtained on that day! And the very first recognition of their independence was that ceremony—which I obtained as the result of my quick maneuvering, and leadership of the group of Western nations in the CSCE—before Washington had even woken up! I did that alone—I did not even have an experienced colleague in my own delegation with whom I could consult, nor experienced counterparts in other Western delegations who could have given me meaningful advice. I just plunged ahead to accomplish the recognition of the independence of those new states, because I saw it as the right thing to do. And now the Ukrainians are fighting and dying to preserve that independence—it is THAT important to them!

What we are currently experiencing is Putin's extraordinary, and baseless, effort to undo history by brazenly seizing control of the independent state of Ukraine and bringing it, by force, back under the control of Russia, in stark contrast to that very moment, years ago, when the world recognized the full, and internationally approved, sovereignty of that independent country, along with all the other "Newly-independent States from the Former USSR".

I am a cynical, old, retired diplomat, and I have seen a lot of international relations over the years. But I believe that day, with the unfolding events it entailed, was a moving, and history-making episode, which deserves some focus and acknowledgement.

Shortly after the dissolution of the USSR, and in the midst of multiple high-level contacts and negotiations between the leaders for the "Newly Independent States from the Former USSR," Secretary of State James Baker, announced—in a speech at Princeton University—that he would send the US Ambassador to the CSCE (myself) as a special envoy to officially and symbolically open direct US diplomatic relations with each of the "Newly Independent States from the Former USSR." Of course, it would have been insulting to these new states to celebrate their independence by sending the American Ambassador in Moscow to mark that independence, and it would also take some time for Washington to officially nominate, and confirm, specific Ambassadors to each of these new countries. New embassies had to be opened, and many other elements had to be sorted out, before true embassies could truly represent the United States in these newly-designated capital cities. There were 12 new countries, including the now-independent state of Russia, and the US had no representative at all in their capitals, with the exception of Russia itself. New embassies had to be found, opened, staffed, etc. So my mission was intended to be a rapid gesture of recognition for these "newly independent" states.

The specific language used with respect to these new states was important, and had to take into account the history which surrounded the USSR and its relations with its neighbors. Some regions of the USSR — particularly the Baltic States — were claimed by Moscow despite strong resistance, but had never been recognized by the USA, and a few other Western countries, as parts of the USSR. In fact, these Baltic States had maintained embassies in Washington throughout the period of their "forced incorporation" into the USSR, and had active lobbying organizations and multiple supporters in the US itself through the diaspora of Baltic States citizens who had migrated to the USA. And there were other aspects of the complex history of the vast regions of what had been the USSR which had to be respected.

The choice of the US Ambassador to the CSCE for such a unique mission was both expedient and symbolic — I was already confirmed by the Senate, which made it possible for me to travel to the region virtually immediately, while avoiding possibly-complicated Ambassadorial confirmation hearings. As a confirmed Ambassador, I already held a position in which I had been dealing with these new states, helping their representatives to assume their roles as new members of the CSCE, and numerous other related issues. This was useful, because nomination of new Ambassadors would require confirmation by the Senate, which would open up a Pandora's Box of complicated issues involving the interests of emigre groups in the US — and possibly other interested groups. The fact that I was already a US Ambassador, confirmed by the Senate, with a mandate and experience which was directly relevant to the situation and the history of the Baltic

States, was thus useful, and vastly simplified my ability to carry out this new mandate immediately.

My unique mission as the first directly-accredited US Ambassador to visit each of these "Newly-Independent States from the former USSR" as independent countries was thus conceived as a symbolic gesture, and also as an expedient which would serve as something of a diplomatic "place holder" until specific individual Ambassadors could be identified, nominated and confirmed by the Senate, and also until appropriate quarters could be found for embryonic US Embassies in each of the new capital cities.

My mission was greeted with interest and pleasure among the informed populations of the newly-designated capital cities I visited, but was not very welcome among the somewhat closed community of "Russian specialists" in the US Foreign Service, who traditionally filled all the positions at the US Embassy in Moscow, as well as the related supporting offices in Washington. This "establishment" of US experts on Russia—who had gained entry into this group only after serious—and lengthy—study of the Russian language and culture, as well as the Soviet governing system—were always suspicious of non-Soviet specialists coming into their area of expertise. In a weird way the American "Russian experts" were almost as hostile to representatives of NATO as they were to the Russians themselves!

In addition, the US Embassy in Moscow had always been the central supervising organization for all official American dealings in the whole of the USSR, and the US diplomats there understood that their role in the vast regions of the USSR would inevitably be reduced by the establishment of separate embassies in each of the component "republics" in what had been the sprawling Soviet Union. There were many such "republics," most with their own languages, histories, and cultures. In some cases, the populations of these regions were not ethnic Russians at all, and some were clearly ethnically Asian, with their own distinct cultures and histories. In some cases, there were historic animosities among them, or between them and Moscow. It should be noted that such "small peoples" (meaning distinct ethnic groups without large numbers of members) still exist in the far-reaching lands of Russia and the

other regions of what was the USSR. Some have their own languages and even, in some cases, elements of self-government—for
example, with respect to issues relating the identity of the "people" or ethnic group involved. This is one of the idiosyncrasies of
the way the USSR was organized, based on the ethnic identities of
these peoples in their scattered homelands.

The US Ambassador in Moscow was particularly uneasy
about the arrival in this region of another US official with the title
of Ambassador and with a special mission relating to these newly-
independent regions, and saw my mission as undercutting and
anticipating a sweeping reduction of his role and authority in
these now-separate-and-independent new States. When I arrived
in Moscow to begin my mission, I was confronted with a certain
degree of hostility emanating from this Ambassador, as well as the
Embassy staff, against which I "pushed back," noting that, while I
had the utmost respect for the role of the Ambassador in Moscow,
I had a new and different role, reflecting the new situation. But
very soon I encountered annoying issues, as the Ambassador personally deleted portions of one of my reporting telegrams to
Washington, without consulting—or even informing—me. And I
only realized this when, by chance, I saw the text of my report as
it had actually been sent—minus some of my text! I asked to see
the Ambassador, and since he was not immediately available, I
left a hand-written message of resentment and objection, noting
that I was an Ambassador too, with my own mission, mandated
directly by the Secretary of State, and that while I recognized his
authority within the Moscow Embassy, I was, like any other Ambassador, responsible directly to Washington. I later managed to
communicate my personal comments to the interested officials.
But since I was only carrying out a one-time mission, my longer-
range view was less emphatic; I thought that, over time, the Ambassadors who were chosen to preside over the new Embassies
which would be established in these newly-recognized countries
would carve out their own areas of primary interest, and their
own relationships with the US Embassy in Moscow. My role was
limited to my symbolic one-time mission to the "newly-independent states from the former USSR," so it was not something to get

excited about. However, this experience provided me with a standpoint from where I could see these historical movements and was able to analyze and later share my recommendations with various audiences.

While I was in the role of the Ambassador who had negotiated the official end of the Cold War, and had returned from a pioneering venture to open direct US diplomatic relations with the newly-independent States from the former USSR, I was invited to be the lead speaker for a seminar at Stanford University, during which I recounted my experience in negotiating with the USSR, and also in my unique mission to the new states in Russia's "Near Abroad." Most of the lecture/seminar series entailed factually recounting of my travel and observations, but of course I also offered my analyses of how the regions of the former USSR were evolving, and their likely evolution in the future. Much of this analysis was rather pessimistic, since I thought it would be difficult for the United States to have any real influence—or even communication—with these distant regions, which were tied up in their past as integral parts of the USSR. I thought, and still believe, that the Russian history and experience of these regions remains as their dominant characteristic, and it will take decades, or even longer, for these newly-independent (and quasi-independent) states to evolve in individual ways. My basic, underlying, and pessimistic, warning was clearly the central theme of this seminar series, and was summed up in a pamphlet issued at that time by the Stanford University Center for International Security and Arms Control, called "The End of the Cold War is Also Over." The text of this summary is included in Annex IV, since it is still relevant to the evolving situation in the region, but this short excerpt discusses the complexity:

> "Just as the Cold War is over, the period known as "the end of the Cold War'" is also over. That brief phase was one of optimism that East and West would finally be united, and would work together to construct a stable and prosperous Europe. Unfortunately, this hope faded rapidly. The turnabout began in late 1992 or the beginning of 1993, as Russia appeared

to turn toward authoritarianism, aggressive nationalism, and an imperial-istic foreign policy". [6]

That essay was based on my "reading" of the state of East-West relations at that time, which was that the "honeymoon" period of more friendly US-Russian relations that had developed under Gorbachev, was over, and that we were back in the traditional stand-off with Moscow which had been the situation throughout the Cold War. So, I named that summary of my lecture series "The End of the Cold War is Also Over".

During my unusual, possibly unique, tenure as the negotiat-ing Ambassador dealing with multiple aspects of those relations, there was a period which seemed to presage better relations with Moscow. Our relations with the Russians at that time had taken on a seemingly positive character, but then, after that brief period, it seemed that we were back to the traditional East-West face-off. That title, "The End of The Cold War is Also Over," was ambigu-ous, which annoyed some Stanford scholars. It reflected the am-biguous character of that period, which posed many problems, new and old, as we started to put aside our brief period of opti-mism and resume, again, all the cautions of the Cold War. But by observing Russian actions, and the aims which Russian negotia-tors have pursued in their dealings with the new states, it was possible to draw up a tentative list of policy directions. As I wrote back then, and especially after two years of war in Ukraine, "based on this crude revival of Kremlinology, the Russians appear to want:

- **Control of the outer frontiers of the whole of the former USSR**. The Russians point out that there were no marked or even surveyed internal borders in the former USSR, and to establish them now would be very costly. By their logic, a better solution is simply to reestablish the old frontiers, and man them with Russian border forces. Cur-rent exceptions to this general rule include the Baltic

---

[6] Summary of series of lectures at Stanford University, "The End of the Cold War Is Also Over", 1995.

states and Azerbaijan, but in the latter case the Russians are actively pressing for reintroduction of their border guards along the frontier with Iran.

- **To maintain military bases throughout the former USSR.** After the Russians forced Eduard Shevardnadze to capitulate and invite Russian forces into Georgia, and after Russia's troops finally agreed to leave the Baltic states of Estonia and Latvia, Russian basing rights are in question only in Azerbaijan, where the government clearly does not want the Russians to return and is resisting strong pressure to agree to the reopening of their large base in Gandzha. The other new states never managed to get rid of the Russians.

- **Control of natural resources throughout the former USSR, particularly energy resources.** Not only does Russia itself need these resources, it also knows that they are a prime source of hard currency, and could enable some former colonies to escape from Russian control. The Russian technique for gaining control over resources is not very subtle: Russia simply demands a share, and insists that pipeline routes from the Caucasus and Central Asia should cross Russia.

- **To keep the international community out.** This means in particular the United States and its surrogates. Russian xenophobes are determined to exclude both American influence and Turkish or Islamic influences, to which Russia is particularly sensitive along its southern frontier.

- Finally, the Russians are determined **to prevent a breakup of the Russian Federation itself,** the "empire within an empire," which includes many colonized peoples. The favored technique for ensuring control over Russia is to reestablish control over the whole of the (former) USSR through consolidation of the Russian-dominated Commonwealth of Independent States (CIS). This would reestablish the traditional buffer zones and theoretically insulate the Russian Federation from such potential instabilities.

All of these neo-imperialist policies have been clearly displayed in Russia's brutal attack on Chechnya. It is of course technically true that Chechnya lies within the borders of the Russian Federation as they are recognized by every other country in the world. But the offensive against Grozny has raised many issues which transcend frontiers, such as the international obligation of all governments to respect the human rights of their citizens. And in the course of the attack Russia has broken its engagements in numerous treaties, including the Treaty on Conventional Forces in Europe (CFE) and the Charter of the United Nations, the Helsinki Final Act, the Charter of Paris for a New Europe, the Agreement on Confidence and Security-Building Measures (CSBMs), and the Summit Document of the Budapest Meeting of the OSCE. Less than two weeks before ordering the attack on Chechnya, Yeltsin himself signed the OSCE Code of Conduct covering, inter alia, how a state deals with internal conflicts. Violating treaty obligations and other international undertakings is a fundamentally international matter—not an "internal" affair. The extraordinary demonstration by Yeltsin's government of neo-imperialism, of dictatorial repression, of brutal disregard for human rights, and of disdain for public opinion in Russia and the world puts the Yeltsin government in the same category as the Soviet regimes of the past. In short, the period known as the "End of the Cold War" has been resoundingly concluded by Russia's attack on Grozny. It is simply no longer possible to speak of a "democratic" government in the Kremlin; democratic governments do not attempt crudely to destroy cities and whole peoples on their own territory. On the contrary, democratic governments are under heavy international obligations to protect their own citizens and their rights. Those in the West who are fond of arguing that unless the West supports Yeltsin it will be faced with "a worse alternative" must face up to the fact that Yeltsin himself is responsible for Grozny; that for the Chechens there is very little that could be "worse" and that the only domestic support for this lunatic venture has come from Vladimir Zhirinovsky himself, everyone's nominal "worse alternative".

The West, particularly the United States, must now develop a much more realistic analysis of Russia and the world as it is in

1995, and as it is likely to evolve into the next century. Such an analysis must form the basis for a new American foreign policy consensus and a coherent, clear and consistent U.S. role in the world. More than anything else, the world needs steady leadership in this rapidly changing period. This leadership must be based on firm moral values and political direction, and only America can provide it".[7]

Some of the Stanford faculty who were present for my lectures rejected or belittled my warnings, and their skeptical comments were included in the pamphlet when it was published. There is, in my view, a natural – and understandable – tendency among university professors to believe that they have a better understanding of international relations than diplomats. A few of them expressed their views guardedly in comments on my lectures, which were included in the pamphlet that published the full text of my presentations. But I think my warnings during my visit to Stanford have proved to be prophetic, and have been amply justified by the very negative evolution of relations with Moscow which we have seen since that time. One of the major conclusions I came to, based on my experience traveling through the distant regions of what had been the USSR, was that the region was, indeed, very remote from the rest of the world – in distance and also in a historic and analytical sense – and that it would take a very long time for this remoteness to evolve. And my experience since then – including my two-year residence in Baku as a visiting professor at a new and very modern university – have only reinforced that impression.

These were my thoughts in 1995 and though much has changed since, the parallels with what Russia did to Chechnya back then and what Russia is doing to Ukraine as this book is written, are startling. The former Soviet space is still struggling with the post-imperial complexity, which led to armed conflicts and exercising military might, rather than openness, acceptance of the new realities and adapting to the demands by the peoples.

---

[7]   Summary of series of lectures at Stanford University, "The End of the Cold War Is Also Over", 1995.

In the 1990's Russia and its former empire, the so-called "near abroad" were going through this struggle which I predicted will probably take years, possibly decades, to complete the transition. All of the features of exodus, bitterness, economic chaos, rear-guard actions, and fratricidal competition have appeared in parts of the former Soviet space, and I argued will surely emerge elsewhere before the process has run its course. Part of that struggle was that there was little agreement in Moscow as to how to retain the "empire," or even whether this is a good idea. Although millions of Russians believed it was a mistake to let the near abroad go, many Russians were also aware that restoring Russia's dominance over these former colonies will also restore Russia's responsibility for them. Each one of them was besieged by complex problems, and the Russian government was already struggling just to keep Russia itself united and economically viable.

But as often happens in periods of difficulty, aggressive nationalism appeared to be winning the debate over the proper role for Russia in the near abroad. As a consequence, there had been no objection to the fact that the defense ministry took the lead in formulating Russia's policies in the former Soviet space ostensibly with the purpose of restoring order and ensuring security on Russia's frontiers.

The Russian defense establishment has been an armed force without a mission since the collapse of Communism, which formed its ideological justification and gave it a purpose. It was positioned, politically and psychologically, to be the defender of the ethnic Russian populations in the newly independent states, and the guarantor of stability everywhere on the territory of the former Soviet Union. The world's image of the Russian armed forces was of a demoralized, underfunded, ill-housed, and unprepared military organization which is no longer a threat to international security. This may be true at the global level, with the important caveat of Russia's nuclear arsenal. But on the territory of the former USSR the Russian army still loomed large even after the dissolution of the USSR. Russia's armed forces had almost two million men under arms, the full range of equipment, and a tough approach to problems which was often reflected in the comments of their leader at the time, Defense Minister Pavel Grachev.[8] Despite the problems encountered in the attack on Grozny, this was a military force which was capable of intervening anywhere in the former USSR, and which has already done so with relative success in Tajikistan, Georgia, and Moldova. The military capacity of the Russian army has changed over time, but it kept some of the interlinked bases, command, control and communications channels, and supply routes throughout ex-Soviet territory. It controlled mountains of weapons and ammunition supplies, plus "volunteers" and cheap mercenaries of every technical specialty. Its officer corps, was a far-flung fraternity that maintained enormous influence in every defense ministry in the newly independent states. Furthermore, the old KGB intelligence and internal security networks were largely intact, and very little could happen in the vast ex-Soviet space without it being known in the defense and internal security ministries in Moscow. The development of the CIS (Commonwealth of Independent States) has helped to provide a facade of international cooperation toward dealing with conflicts within the former USSR. Russia has also tried to obtain international acceptance of the CIS as an organization equivalent to, say, the European Union. It argued that the CIS had exclusive competence for dealing with conflicts on the territory of the former USSR. In cases which have elicited international interest, such as Georgia, Azerbaijan, and Tajikistan, the Russians have made a point of calling their proposed peacekeeping interventions CIS operations, even when participation by non-Russian CIS members was no more than symbolic. All CIS operations would, of course, be dominated or possibly even exclusively manned by Russia. The military and its backers like to think of all their operations in the so-called "near abroad" as peacekeeping, and apparently believe that they should be backed and even paid for by the international community at large. But the Russians have developed their own

---

8   See, for example, Grachev's statement before a negotiating session on Nagor-no-Karabakh that "Whatever I propose, that's what we're going to agree on," cited in Elizabeth Fuller, "The Karabakh Mediation Process; Grachev versus the CSCE?" *R.FEIRL Research Report,* Vol. 3, No. 23, June 10, 1994.

concept of peacekeeping which is quite different from the classic definition, and which contrasts sharply, not only with the longstanding practices of the United Nations in this field, but also with normal relations among independent states.

The Russian concept of peacekeeping[9] is really more like forceful suppression of violence than it is like the impartial and pacific approach of international organizations. Even the expression, when used in Russian, means something different. Concretely, Russian troops engaged in such operations are authorized to use force not only to defend themselves if they are attacked, but also to suppress violations of the peace, whatever the cause. UN peacekeeping missions are only authorized to use force in self-defense. Russian peacekeeping also does not put the same stress on the negotiation of stable political solutions as is the case in international operations. Suppression of violence is itself a goal. For the international community peacekeeping is only an unavoidable expedient which may help to make it possible to organize a rational political negotiation to find a resolution to the underlying dispute. In this approach the goal is clearly the achievement of a negotiated political solution, not just the suppression of violence. The Russian approach grows naturally out of the historical experience of the Russian and Soviet armed forces with respect to security problems within the USSR. When such problems arose, the army was sent to impose order. They often accomplished this objective brutally, and in some cases the legacy they left behind only complicated and embittered the underlying dispute. Many historians contend that in fact the deliberate policy of Stalin was to keep local hostilities alive, or even to create or fuel them, in order to ensure that distant parts of the Soviet Union would always be dependent on the Center for their security.

A part of the dilemma for the West has always been the possibility that Russian peacekeeping troops would use intimidation

---

[9]   "Russia's 'Near Abroad' — a Dilemma for the West" by John Maresca. First Published in: "Crisis Management in the CIS: Whither Russia?" Hans-Georg Ehrhart, Anna Kreikemeyer and Andrei V. Zagorski, eds. © Nomos Verlagsgesellschaft, Baden-Baden, 1995. Reprinted with kind permission in "Helsinki Revisited".

or force to suppress elements they considered unfavorable to Moscow's interests, just as Soviet forces did before them. Coupled with the Russian interpretation of their peacekeeping role is a strongly-held view that maintaining peace and stability on the territory of the former USSR is the exclusive prerogative of Russia. This view, too, resembles the possessive attitudes of virtually all colonial powers with respect to their former colonies, but is perhaps felt even more strongly in the case of Russia because of the country's historic xenophobia, particularly toward the West. Many Russians see their country as having a unique role across Eurasia, and do not believe outsiders have any place in this area. Russian suspicions of outside attempts to settle problems in the former USSR have come out most strongly in the behavior of Russian representatives with regard to the conflict over the mountain enclave of Nagorno-Karabakh, in the Trans-Caucasus. This is because this is the one conflict on former Soviet territory in which an international body—the "Minsk Group"—has been mandated to find a solution. Here the Russians, led by defense minister Grachev, have made a concerted effort to undercut international initiatives, to keep the international community out, and to resolve the problem themselves, using their own troops, as a way of ensuring their domination of the region. The Russians have appeared prepared to accept accusations of bad faith in this instance, as the price of ensuring exclusive Russian predominance".[10]

Kozyrev's "Mock Speech" in Stockholm reveals Moscow's real intentions in the Near Abroad

If there was a moment—a single moment—when I realized that Russia was starting what would become a very long, largely patient, multi-facetted attempt to recover its forceful grip over all of its colonized territories, inherited from the empire of the Czars, it was in Stockholm in December of 1992. It was, very precisely, during Russian Foreign Minister Andrei Kozyrev's "mock speech" to

---

[10]   The full text can be found as Annex 6.

a meeting of the foreign ministers of the CSCE member states. Kozyrev's speech was nothing less than an aggressive, toughly-worded statement of Russia's intention to reclaim what it deemed to be its rightful domination over all the vast European and Asian territories which had—until quite recently, when the USSR was officially dissolved—been parts of the Russian Empire, and later of the Soviet Union.

His comments with respect to the "near abroad" were particularly harsh; Kozyrev asserted that 'The space of the former Soviet Union cannot be viewed as a zone where the CSCE norms can be applied in full. This is in effect a post-imperial space where Russia has to defend its interests by all available means, including military and economic ones. We shall firmly insist that the former republics of the USSR immediately join the new federation or confederation, and this will be discussed in no uncertain terms.' This was an extraordinary assertion at that time—shortly after the official dissolution of the USSR—so extraordinary that, as I wrote in my 2016 book "Helsinki Revisited," reporters began to run to the doors to send urgent dispatches to their home offices, for the next editions. And Kozyrev himself clearly realized that he may have been a bit too frank in his statement, and took the floor again, dramatically, to say that "it was all a joke"—just a good-natured way of informing all the leaders of Europe and North America who were assembled at this meeting of the Foreign Ministers of the member countries of the CSCE what Russia's position "might be" if it were not so reasonable, statesman-like, etc. He had obviously been informed that journalists were rushing to the phones, and delegations were sending off urgent cables to their capitals, alarmed by his hard-line warning.

But what we now know is just the opposite; Kozyrev's "mock speech" in Stockholm was a brief glimpse of the Russian dream—and of the Kremlin's concrete plan—to re-cover the lands of the "Near Abroad," which had started to slip away with the "temporary" dissolution of the USSR. It was deemed necessary to allow this slippage to start, so as to sound the alarm in Moscow, and thus to justify getting rid of the troublesome Gorbachev, who was simply too "westernizing" to be acceptable to Moscow's hard liners, and who had put Moscow's long-time control over the whole of the ancient Russian empire into jeopardy.

I first reported Kozyrev's "mock" speech, and its significance, in an article quoted above, which I published in 1995, titled "Russia's Near Abroad; a Dilemma for the West". It was included as a chapter in an obscure book called "Crisis Management in the CIS: Whither Russia." Such articles were considered very radical at the time, and could only be published in minor publications. But now they appear positively prescient, because we all know — now — that this was, indeed, the Russian game-plan all along. The plan of the KGB, and its hard-line backers and supporters, was — and still is — the plan which Putin is trying to implement and carry out now, many years later, on behalf of his life-long agency, the KGB, and its successor, now called the FSB. It is simply amazing how blind the West has been — all these years — as Putin prepared his coup! Of course, such a plan does not seem very logical or even feasible to rational westerners, but it reflects the complex thinking of Kremlin insiders.

But now we have seen Putin's plan unfold in Ukraine, without much success, leading him to turn to ever more radical measures. And he has done this, as is always his style, in the "Russian way" — a mixture of dramatic, random bombing of civilian targets and shocking, unspeakable brutality wherever the Russian army gains control, with threats of even worse treatment to come. This was the tactic followed by the Russians when their forces swept into Germany at the end of the Second World War — justified by Moscow at the time on the grounds that their army was simply avenging the brutality of the Nazi invasion of Russia. And later on, it was the strategy for quelling the uprising in Chechnya, which is still fresh in the memories of all the peoples of the former USSR. Such tactics are inexcusable in any circumstances, but are outrageous in the current situation of Ukraine. Unfortunately, they are also normal, regular options in the KGB/FSB playbook.

Before 1993 was over, Kozyrev's "real" policies closely resembled the hard-line nationalist policies of his "mock" Stockholm speech. In particular, Russia's determination to regain control over as much as possible of the former USSR had become obvious to all but the most naive Western observers. Some analysts have suggested that the Yeltsin government adjusted its policies because of the electoral strength shown by Vladimir Zhirinovsky, a virulent nationalist, in the Russian parliamentary elections in the autumn of 1993. While this made the world conscious of the nationalist trend in Russia, in fact the evolution of policy began much earlier. The appearance of Zhirinovsky merely revealed the growing depth and breadth of nationalist feeling as Russia progressed through a period of economic and political retrenchment. The general state of disarray in Moscow made it difficult to find an authoritative statement of Russian foreign policy, particularly in the critical area of the newly independent states of the former USSR. Maybe there was not a centrally developed or approved policy concept or policy objectives. Rather, foreign policy may have reflected an accumulation of separate actions by different ministries, all seeking to anticipate what they see as the tendency of political opinion.

War over Nagorno Karabakh

The ancient confrontation between the Armenians of this remote and mountainous region and the Azerbaijanis who compose the population of the sovereign State which surrounds it, became active when the two states involved — Armenia and Azerbaijan — became independent following the dissolution of the Soviet Union. Significantly, the strangely-tortured boundaries between these two states — officially fixed just after the Russian revolution by a traveling, Moscow-commissioned boundary committee chaired by Joseph Stalin himself — have ensured the bloody, ongoing, dispute between them since that time, making into one of the most prominent "internal" conflicts in the area of the former USSR. The unavoidable conclusion from this history is that the new post-revolution Communist regime in Moscow intentionally maintained the bases for on-going disputes over the border, ensuring continuing conflict between the two long-standing ethnic enemies. Russia, which still maintains a military base in Armenia and also controls the sensitive border between both former Soviet republics and the neighboring state of Iran, wants to keep foreigners out, even if they might help to resolve the war. Maintaining its exclusive role as the arbiter of local wars is very useful for Russia, since it makes both sides in a conflict — in this case Azerbaijan and Armenia — dependent on Moscow's military forces, its ability to intervene rapidly in this "near abroad" region, its training and equipment, as well as its carefully-limited efforts to reduce or conclude the conflict.

I was plunged into the Nagorno-Karabakh conflict as a result of my role as an itinerant American Ambassador visiting each of the "newly independent states." Both official sides in this dispute sought my understanding and support, and I tried to find a pathway to negotiations and some form of peaceful resolution. But the Armenian community in the USA is very active politically — which exposed me to considerable harassment at a time when Armenian activists were carrying out bloody attacks and assassinations, and both sides resisted any concessions. My efforts to develop a negotiating process which might lead to a peaceful resolution were fruitless, despite my many visits to the region, private discussions with national leaders, and meetings with lobbying groups from both sides. Even now, more than a quarter of a century after the breakup of the USSR, the confrontation in the region is still very active, includes periodic episodes of bloody conflict, and there are no indications of peaceful possibilities. I testified before a committee of the US Congress on this general subject when I was actively pursuing some sort of cease-fire between the parties to this conflict, and a report of my testimony was included at pp. 231-236 of my book, "Helsinki Revisited."

The future of Russia's "Near Abroad" — and what is at stake in this vast region — depends on the evolution of conflicts in a number of places, including Nagorno Karabakh, Georgia, Grozny and, of course, Ukraine. But there are many other parts of the former regions of the USSR where opposition to Moscow's rigid control is suppressed. Russia has gradually tightened its grip on these regions, partly to forestall possible conflict resolution efforts by outsiders in any part of its so-called "Near Abroad". Russia—at least the government of Vladimir Putin—considers the whole of the territory of the former USSR to be an "exclusion zone" for any activities or support from other countries. In addition, Moscow has used its traditional multiple-solutions approach to insert itself in a variety of ways, to make local governments and communities dependent on specific services which only Russia can realistically offer in these remote regions. Moscow's strategy of carefully-rationed support is habit-forming, and over time it becomes the easiest way for weak regional governments to deal with problems.

Some years ago I published an essay on the broad issue of ethnic groups in the territories of the former USSR—called "Foreign Devils on the Silk Road—Take Two." It was published (in Chinese) in a Chinese periodical called the "China International Strategy Review," in 2015. There are, of course, many ethnic groups scattered throughout the territory of the former USSR, and many of these groups, especially those in the Central Asian part of this vast region, are related to ethnic groups in China itself. China has an interest in these neighboring regions, and follows developments in them very closely.

Of course the regions of the former USSR which are near to Europe are easier to understand as parts of the Russian identity — its legitimate lands. The farther East one travels the more remote Moscow becomes; the local heritages are more prominent, and Russian elements seem increasingly foreign. This is a key factor in the region, and should not be automatically dismissed, despite the fact that these regions are little-known to the West, including the USA. But Moscow ruled these regions for a very long time, and it is difficult to imagine them becoming fully independent of Russian domination. The current situation—consisting of a superficial-but-important Russian component in the local hierarchical structure, and a dominant Russian role in key decision-making — is likely to continue, along with the networks of key governing agencies which lead back to Moscow. Those structures will be maintained ... in the "Russian way."

Russia's Military Efforts in the Near Abroad are closely connected with the personality of Putin

He relishes confrontation and loves to maintain his hardline image. He has increasingly stressed that the entire area of the former USSR is a special-interest region for Russia, hinting at his readiness to expand local wars, using scandalous and unacceptable techniques of intimidation and violence, as he did in Grozny and Georgia, and has now also done in Ukraine (plus other regions). In view of my past experience in the region, I have followed these activities closely, and they have reached a shameful peak in Ukraine. The West must urgently develop a far stronger strategy — and new technical capabilities — for countering this type of Russian activity, which can only be compared with some of Hitler's tactics during World War Two. Local leaders who are willing to stand up to Moscow need encouragement, support, and, in some cases, actual protection. And the Russians who are responsible, and are enabling Putin — chiefly the Russian billionaire class — must be held accountable, along with Putin himself. We need new tactics, techniques, and technologies for punishing them directly and personally when they cross the line of legitimate international engagement.

In a text titled "Countering Putin's "Near Abroad" Strategy", posted on European Leadership Network website since January 9, 2020, I explained in more detail the geopolitical implications of the current developments, and I offered a suggested response by the USA and Europe. As I said back then, Americans and Europeans have not yet fully realized that what is happening in Ukraine is just one part of Russian President Vladimir Putin's broader strategy for what Russians call their "near abroad." The immediate focus is on the Black Sea-Caspian region, the Caucasus and Central Asia, the heart of the "near abroad." Putin's overall objective is to take back as much as possible of the full territory of the former USSR, by whatever means might be successful. This will be done in the Russian way — through a variety of control mechanisms, association agreements, stationing of forces, or whatever else creates leverage to control the governments of these vast regions.

The Western response should therefore be strategic, designed to counter both the immediate challenges in Ukraine, and this broader Russian scheme. The aim is to ensure the independence of the former USSR states, and to keep the current narrow corridor from Europe across the Black Sea and the Caucasus to Central Asia open. This must be a key objective for the United States and Europe, for without it the entire Eurasian continent north of the Himalayas will be controlled by Russia and China, with Western access only possible with the consent of one of these powers.

Of course, Central Asia and the Caucasus are distant from the key priorities of the West. Or are they? The US and NATO could not have supplied their military forces in Afghanistan during the 9/11 war there without transit routes through this vast region, and the Central Asian/Caucasus gas and oil transiting in current or planned pipelines are essential for Europe. In addition, many Western companies are helping to develop the region. So Central Asia and the Caucasus are not as distant from Western concerns as some might like to think. Moreover, economic growth in this vast region will affect many aspects of the world's economy, so it is not some distant consideration.

Although most of the world did not notice, the sporadic gunfire which has been exchanged between the armies of Armenia and Azerbaijan has ratcheted up in parallel with events in Ukraine. These countries have faced each other in hostility for the last twenty years in the hills of western Azerbaijan, following the seizure of almost twenty percent of Azerbaijan's territory by Russian-supported Armenian troops. Putin convened a meeting of the Presidents of Armenia and Azerbaijan in Sochi—his way of showing the world that the Caucasus is within Russia's region of influence, and of making sure the countries of the region know that it is Russia which encourages or terminates sputtering conflicts in the near abroad, when it wishes to do so. This is also the situation in Eastern Ukraine, in case any Westerners have not understood—Russia can end the fighting when it wishes, and it will do so when it has recuperated its basic leverage on the government of Ukraine.

As we have known, but somehow left aside in pure naiveté, Russia considers it's so-called "near abroad" a part of its national identity, its vital interests, and its natural area of control. In an essay published twenty years ago by an institute at the University of Hamburg[11], I pointed this out very clearly, and warned of the problems we are now facing, starting with Crimea. Russia will respond with the usual complex Russian maneuvers when it considers that its control over these vast regions is somehow threatened. This is in the Russian culture—a variety of small efforts, each of a somewhat different nature, confuses the opponent. The West's inherent need for absolute clarity plays into Russia's hands. Moscow's maneuvers will almost never be clearly aggressive, and the military units involved will usually not be clearly identifiable as Russian troops. Ambiguity and a variety of small, seemingly unrelated moves are not coincidental, nor are the efforts of small "volunteer" groups supposedly acting on their own. These initiatives are part of a coherent plan; they constitute the strategy. Vladimir Putin is a master of it, and he always keeps a poker face.

Confronted with this situation, the West must develop a new strategy of its own. It is not enough to invoke economic sanctions which hurt western countries as much as they do Russia, or to announce the creation of rapid-deployment units. Putin's challenge is broad and many-faceted, and the response must be shaped to meet this new challenge. Just as NATO for years faced Soviet tanks with its own in Germany, the Western Allies must develop effective responses to this new sort of threat. A Russia which is seeking to re-establish control over the former Soviet space must

---

[11]   'Russia's "Near Abroad" — A Dilemma for the West,' by John J. Maresca, chapter in "Crisis Management in the CIS: Whither Russia," Hans-Georg Ehrhart, Anna Kriekemeyer and Andrei V. Zagorski, eds., Institut fur Friedensforschung und Sicherheitspolitik, Hamburg University, 1995.

be considered as a challenge to the very notion of a free and democratic Europe.[12]

The Need to Truly Isolate, and Inflict Pain on Russia ... and Putin!

We need to take steps far beyond the current efforts; steps which will truly isolate and impose real economic and political pain on Russia, especially on Russia's so-called "elites." For example, furnishing missiles to Ukraine which can be used to target infrastructure in Russia, to enable Ukraine to mount a symmetrical response to Russia's current attacks on Ukraine with the ability to reach distant targets, and confiscating Russian-owned assets in Western countries, to be sold to finance the war against Russia. Also, we need to provide Ukraine with a full range of specific defensive weapons, which may need to be developed more rapidly! This will be challenging — even difficult — but we cannot stand by idly while Putin destroys a neighboring state thru a continuing barrage of missiles aimed at civilians and civilian targets — without enabling Ukraine with effective and meaningful weapons to use in response. Putin cannot be permitted to continue his war on Ukraine with impunity.

---

[12] "Countering Putin's "Near Abroad" Strategy", posted on European Leadership Network website, https://www.europeanleadershipnetwork.org/comm entary/countering-putins-near-abroad-strategy/

EPILOGUE–
WHAT CAN THE OSCE DO TO HELP END
THE WAR IN UKRAINE

The CSCE's peak was probably that meeting in Paris, and unfortunately for the CSCE, and for Europe, there are a lot of other things that have now taken place. The CSCE had its day and was important at the time, but it is no longer relevant, now. If someone tomorrow proposes a new summit-level session of the CSCE to resolve the problem of Ukraine then maybe, suddenly, it could take center stage again. But nobody is doing that, and it is hard to imagine—where would it be, to begin with? It would have to be somewhere in the middle to symbolically fit that role, and who would host it? Would the Turks do that, for example? Would they offer to hold such a conference in Istanbul? Without some new lift-off like that the OSCE is irrelevant today.

The issues are different now, there has been an incredible amount of destruction and mindless, deliberate cruelty. And the dangers of a wider, more destructive war, are more present than ever before. So, the CSCE is not very relevant to the situation of today. For example, the huge, all-European participation would look very strange—the mini-states, for example. Perhaps we are in circumstances where people start to think in terms of some kind of device that could be used to bring us back to reason, but I don't think Putin cares about anything like that anymore. He is just destroying things—killing people, including women and children—completely randomly! And probably Western leaders do not think Putin should be saved by giving him a way out. In fact, he should NOT be given a way out—he should just disappear! After what he has done, only his disappearance will permit a return to normal East-West relations in Europe. And Russia's role needs to be re-examined, very radically and fundamentally. I don't think the CSCE's institutions can really survive the barbaric nature of this war, which Putin has—unilaterally, personally, deliberately— imposed on Europe.

In the early days of the CSCE one of the factors, which was always a consideration when we started thinking about how things would go in such a body, was how close we were at any given moment to actual combat, to having a war. And I think history has shown that you can only get to the kind of discussions that we have had in the CSCE over time if you are relatively far away from fighting an actual war. Whereas right now we are not only close to having a war, we are actually engaged in a very vicious and destructive war. The idea of having some kind of meaningful dialogue in the midst of killing people – including women and children, destroying cities, sending hundreds of thousands of people fleeing from random destruction – is very remote, very difficult to imagine. Let's face it: Putin is directly and personally responsible for the destruction and cruelty of this war, and he must face the consequences before it will be possible to discuss peace with Russia! We have war crimes tribunals for such crimes, for such wanton destruction! And so right now, I think it is not the time for some sort of bland return to the earlier situation.

Maybe that time will come. Maybe – if there were to be some kind of a practical settlement of the war, and the destruction, the killings of people, even children, were to fade into history, tensions were to be eased over time – and Putin himself were to disappear – it might be possible to get back to a situation where you could have more of a dialogue, and all the things that the CSCE can do might become relevant again. But we are certainly not there now, and whether we will ever get back to those kinds of relations with Russia is very difficult to contemplate right now. However, if there is a renewed interest in seeking more positive relations with Russia, at least in areas where mutual benefits are possible, western leaders would do well to bear in mind the lessons of the détente era of the 1970s. The Soviets have had ample opportunity to demonstrate a good faith effort to carry out their Helsinki Commitments, but no one could contend that they have made a serious effort in this direction. There may be other possibilities for paper agreements in the years ahead, but their value must be judged in the light of this experience. To reach new agreements when previous accords have not yet been implemented can only be misleading and illusory for both sides.

From its beginning the CSCE has benefitted from ideas and innovation and an unusual ability to adjust and respond to current needs. The tradition must be maintained and expanded. If we believe in the values represented by the Helsinki Final Act, we must continue to work for their advancement and full respect.[1]

In addition, we face a whole new international context following Putin's open aggression on Ukraine. That has signaled a willingness to carry out extraordinary, completely uncalled-for violence in pursuit of the conquest of a neighboring sovereign state, which the world has not seen since Hitler's time. This raises the "Putin problem" to one of world-wide consequence and urgency. The UN simply cannot deal with such a problem, because the country which has created this problem has veto power in the UN! The UN structure is antique, and carefully structured to ensure the continuing prominence of Russia. If there were any sensible approach to these things—which there won't be, because it's all politicized—one would update the whole structure and the way it operates, so that everything could be upgraded and modernized. But that will not happen because some countries will resist changes that might reduce their independence. And in the case of Russia, of course it has the power of the "veto" at its disposal (as does the USA), and that makes it impossible to do anything, or to adopt any language, in the UN, which Russia does not approve.

So unfortunately the world—especially the NATO allies and our friends in other parts of the world—will have to go back to the basics of international relations, and start a process of isolating Russia and Putin, perhaps for a very long time, in a kind of "New Cold War." The objectives of this isolation should be to encourage Russia to change course, to end its use of violence to enforce its

---

[1]   John J. Maresca "Ensuring CSCE Promises are Kept", 1995. First published in: Bulletin of the OSCE Office for Democratic Institutions and Human Rights (ODIHR), Vol.3, No.3, Warsaw. ODIHR grants permission to use for educational and non-commercial purposes.

will on its neighbors, and to seek true acceptance by the World Community. Countries which support the Russian position in this situation will have to be subjected to the same isolation as is imposed on Russia. This type of approach is not very effective, but it is the best way of responding to unacceptable behavior without actually starting a war.

Over the longer term I think we need to consider new and creative ways to encourage more normal international behavior by Russia, and to impose really meaningful sanctions when Russia (or any other country) discards so completely the norms of peaceful international relations. As difficult as it may be, we need to construct an international system which can actually enforce the rules of peaceful international behavior. Experience over time has shown how difficult it is to obtain meaningful international commitments which cannot simply be ignored when a country decides to do that.

Afterword

History will remember the current war in Ukraine as an outrageous attempt by Vladimir Putin to recover Russian control over its nearest neighboring State through a savage, bloody and unscrupulous war, conducted largely against the civilian population, the towns and buildings of an innocent country. It will be recorded as one of the most brutal and mindless aggressions of modern history, in which Putin's army, air force and navy have destroyed even the most innocent of targets, with the responsibility resting entirely on Putin.

The whole world has watched this deliberate and senseless destruction — on films and even live television, with close-ups of the cruelty and barbarism of the Russian tactics. The world is well aware of Putin's personal responsibility, and of his military forces' deliberate choices of the most despicable and brutal measures, in their execution of his war on Ukraine. The entire Russian nation has been shamed before the world, by this "Putin" ... and his very name will henceforth "live in infamy" in the history of our time.

The West must find a way to end this senseless war, with Ukraine whole and safe, and with Putin himself suffering the consequences he disserves: nothing less can be an acceptable ending to this horrific blight on the history of our time, and on the legacy of the proud Russian people.

John J. Maresca,
United States Ambassador, retired
Former Special US Envoy to Open United States Diplomatic Relations with the Newly-Independent States, following the dissolution of the Former USSR.

PART II

Interview with Ambassador John Maresca

Conducted by: Ida Manton

Introduction

John J. Maresca is a former American diplomat who was closely involved in the preparations and negotiations leading to the Helsinki Final Act (HFA), signed on August 1, 1975. He was following the preparation of the Conference for Security and Cooperation in Europe as a Deputy Head of the United States Delegation which negotiated the HFA and later as an Ambassador and Head of the US Delegation which negotiated the "Charter of Paris for a New Europe". But even before the Helsinki process, John Maresca was following the intense consultations on how to open discussions and eventually negotiations with the Soviet Union in order to lower the military confrontation and to ease tensions between NATO and the Warsaw Pact while he was Deputy Director of NATO Secretary General's Office. He is one of the key participants who witnessed the processes that created the CSCE in the 1970s and transformed it into an organization in the 1990s.

We have to be grateful for his undertaking to put a lot of what happened in writing and to give us an opportunity to learn from and about that historic period. In addition to the chronicles, the particular value of his publications is the skill with which he weaves the narration, which is something that only a well-versed diplomat with a very attentive approach and strategic mind, can provide, as he was noticing every detail during the processes.

His work and written recollections about parts of the CSCE/OSCE history have inspired research and projects which aim at collecting the memories of negotiators who were creating and building up the structures for sustainable peace and security-and-confidence-building measures. An oral history project, titled

"Living memories", which has been coordinated under the umbrella of the OSCE's Documentation Center in Prague, has a shorter version of this interview. More interviews and information about the project can be found on the OSCE website: www.osce.org.

John Maresca's previous publications on these topics have been a true inspiration for younger researchers and academics, and his knowledge and experience, as well as the conviction about the way forward are a valuable contribution to the current political debate. The OSCE's "Living memories" interviews, including the one with Ambassador Maresca, capture crucial moments of our collective history, that might be of help to those who will be working on post-conflict reconstruction in Ukraine, as they should have in mind some of the lessons learned by people who have walked in their shoes and built structures that Putin blatantly ignored and undermined with the invasion of Ukraine.

This interview is a contribution with focus not only on the history of the CSCE/OSCE, but also on the future of the European security structure and peacebuilding efforts that will be undertaken by the next-generation leaders but also researchers, political scientists and civil society. Probably among those who will read this interview there will be a few who will look up his books: "To Helsinki", "Helsinki Revisited" or the latest one "The Unknown Peace Agreement" (published in April 2022).

Hopefully this interview will be useful to current decision-makers in Vienna and their respective capitals as the OSCE is in a critical situation which requires wisdom in order to preserve it. John Maresca spent more than twenty years of his diplomatic career on building up the structure that was set to relax the tensions between the East and the West and to contribute to maintaining peace. He is among those who can justifiably say they led the greatest moments of the entire history of the organization and when he retired, he left it with permanent on-going and functional institutions that gave life to the CSCE.

In the introduction to "Helsinki Revisited, Maresca writes: "Forty years after it was agreed at Helsinki, the central guideline that any changes in frontiers must take place 'by peaceful means and by agreement', remains the key to enduring peace in the European region. When this rule breaks down, or is ignored, the consequences can be disastrous for the people concerned". This rule has been ignored by Russia in Ukraine and it seems that we are not yet able to see the way out or agree on how to manage the conflict in order to minimize the consequences. It is unlikely that we will reach the peak of hope many diplomats lived through between Helsinki and Paris, but with the interview we offer as part of this book, we hope to shed some light on possible venues and the importance of multilateral diplomacy as a platform for inclusive dialogue.

Mr. Maresca, let us start with Helsinki. In such a polarized world somehow, the circumstances developed to negotiate the Final Act. When you see it from this perspective do you consider it to be a well-crafted and successfully negotiated document or more of a miracle?

I do think it was something of a miracle. My own take on this is that the people who were there in the beginning were thinking differently, but over time they have developed a kind of joint current of just wanting to get something done. None of us wanted to have spent a year or two there, and have produced nothing. Even though that something would be different on each side, the desire to produce something was common to everybody. But before getting there we went through a very long period of just butting heads against each other. Even afterwards there were periods like that, but the commonality of wanting to accomplish something did have an effect, and that was what eventually pushed us along.

I've had this impression of mine confirmed over time by Kovalev, who was a real hardliner, and was always taking a very tough line. Much later in life, he sent me his memoirs.[1] I received them...over a fax. He simply put it into the fax machine, so when

---

[1]   Anatoly Kovalev: "Looking back on the Helsinki Final Act", excerpt from the memoirs of Anatoly Kovalev, published in Transition Magazine by the Open Media Research Institute, Prague, 30 June 1995. ©John J.Maresca.

it arrived at my Radio Liberty office in Prague it was just one long reel of paper which kept coming off the machine. The people in my office who ran this machine were astonished by this. It was all coming off in Cyrillic, which is how he wrote naturally. He wanted me to publish it, so I didn't know what to do with it. I asked the Russian language experts in my Radio Free Europe/Radio Liberty office to look and tell me what they thought of it. They selected and translated some interesting parts, which I later published in our monthly magazine. That was, I think a very interesting experience, because in Kovalev's Memoir of the HFA negotiations I found out what he was thinking during that period, and that's when I learned that the Russians who were there had the same frustrations that we had, that we were both desperately trying to find some little bits and pieces that we could put together in order to have some form of success after all that work.

So, to come back to what I was saying earlier, I think that all of us there, by the time we got down to business, were desperately interested in finding something that we could produce out of these diametrically opposed positions and I think that came through in the document and that is why some parts look a little strange, but it does contain some bits and pieces which were for that period very interesting and a big step forward.

The negotiation outcome often depends on who are the people around the table and I am sure that if there were other people in the delegations, that document would have looked different. But Helsinki was not as enthusiastic and euphoric as Paris was. While Helsinki was maybe a problem-solving exercise in which many constructive, creative diplomats, as you said, wanted to have something done, Paris had a different energy. What made the work of all those diplomats effective and constructive? Was it a special, rather new recipe, a "CSCE model of diplomacy"? Do you consider the Helsinki process to be more effective way of conducting diplomacy or the structures that were created in Paris should have provided for a better platform for dialogue?

In the first days it was very formal, very distant especially between the two opposing blocks, because there were two. There was NATO and the Warsaw Pact, and they were very much opposed blocks with very different, rigid views, subject to group agreements. What was certainly a great advantage in terms of making any progress was the neutrals and non-aligned. They gradually realized that they had a responsibility for pushing things along and became a block of their own. They had some very good people and became a kind of engine pushing us forward because they began to see the whole negotiation as dependent on them to find some middle ground, and they did that very effectively. They would find the necessary words. There were situations where we would argue over a single word for weeks and then the neutrals would come in with alternative words, often even a whole list of words to choose from. Eventually we would find some kind of word that both sides could accept. So, I think the neutrals played a very important role, probably much more important than they got credit for. Without them I think we would never have reached an agreement.

Later, when we were preparing for the CSCE summit in Paris, the situation was quite different. The leader of the USSR was Gorbachev, who was a very rational person and I think was genuinely looking for ways to create a more positive relationship with the West. And he found a like-minded person in Mitterrand, a socialist who was actively looking for ways to build closer relations with the USSR. Mitterrand had deliberately included communists in his first government, as a way of showing his independence while confirming his leftist credentials and actually weakening his communist rivals by taking-over their long-time role in French politics. And he sought closer relations with the USSR thru the moderate Gorbachev. At that time, I was the senior expert on France in the State Department as the Director of relations with Western Europe. Many Americans — business leaders and other prominent persons — came to see me to ask for my analysis of how Europe was evolving. Americans were concerned that France under Mitterrand, who had included French communists in his government, was getting too close to the Russians.

But I knew France pretty well, and I knew Mitterrand personally, and I understood his game. He was playing French politics, to ensure the support of French communist voters, while avoiding any real concessions to the Communist Party. He knew that many French Socialist voters would be hesitant about participation by the Communists in the government of France. So, Mitterrand brought a few Communists into minor positions in his government, and built up his public friendship with Gorbachev, and with this strategy he managed to become closer to Russia while sidelining his domestic rivals on the left—the French Communist Party.

Getting Gorbachev to Paris was a double win, politically, for Mitterrand, and gave him a leadership role among the whole European group. But it doomed Gorbachev. Moscow hardliners viewed him as too "Westernising," and soon we saw Boris Yeltsin withdraw Russia from the Soviet Union—the USSR—in order to eliminate Gorbachev, who was left without any meaningful position. Russia was the very heart of the USSR! And at the same time Yeltsin introduced Putin as his successor. Russia's future course was fixed: Putin, with his crucial ties to the KGB, was mandated to re-assemble Russia's dominance over the whole of what had been the USSR—his life-long mission. And that is what has been playing out, before our eyes, all these years—the attempted, KGB-assisted, re-establishment of Moscow's full control over the whole of what was the USSR. With just one hold-out—but an important one—called ... Ukraine.

Toxic polarization is defining many political processes nowadays. Can we still find countries that will have the respect of both sides and could mediate without taking a side? How can we recreate what you are saying was the core ingredient in the CSCE negotiations—the engine for problem-solving? Is this the main ingredient that we're missing today?

Diplomats have a special problem-solving mentality. I think that even now if you put diplomats together and said: "you have to find something that you all agree on in this subject area" and just made them stay there until they came up with something, they would indeed come up with something. Might be more difficult, might be different from what it was then, but they would produce some result, and the neutrals once again would step in and try to help. That's a methodology which just grew out of nothing because we were forced to do it. In Dipoli nobody really knew what to do next and gradually some themes developed that were just organizational. The idea of baskets, for example, was a big step forward. It sounds ridiculous now, but until the idea emerged of having baskets, we didn't know how to organize the different views. So, these different subject areas, like information, human rights or military things, became baskets containing related ideas and the various views of the different factions, were just put into that basket. They weren't at all the same, and gradually we were able to break them down further within the basket. Whatever the subject was, you could put them together, and gradually you could compare one sentence with another and realize that the positions were quite different, but we had to try to marry them up and that is when the neutrals became indispensable because they would then offer alternative suggestions of how to combine an idea from Moscow and an idea from Washington into a sentence that would seemingly take care of both.

Also, everybody was under pressure. That's another crucial factor. The Russians were under tremendous pressure because it was believed that the initiative came from Russia. People dispute that, and historically it is a question mark of where the initiative came from for this kind of negotiation. I got into this earlier when I was working in NATO for an Italian Secretary General. We already had packages of proposals that they wanted to put forward, because NATO was thinking of something, not exactly like this, but some kind of exchanges with Moscow. NATO took the first step towards some kind of a negotiation by making a public statement that they were appointing an explorer—a representative who would explore options for areas where we might have some kind of common ideas in order to get something started. That was the NATO proposal for getting something started. They even selected the Explorer, an outgoing Secretary General who I worked for, Manlio Brosio.

To answer your question about "the neutrals now," my reply would start with the situation of Russia under Putin. He has deliberately chosen the role of the world's unscrupulous villain, and by doing that he has made it very difficult for any country to be neutral! How can one be neutral in the face of Putin's style of government, his loud threats, his deliberate bullying, his mindless killing of people—even children—targeting of schools and civilian shelters, his destruction of towns and cities—and, worst of all, his senseless invasion of Ukraine? He has created such a toxic situation around him that two of the long-time, traditionally-neutral countries of Europe—his nearby neighbors, Finland and Sweden—have decided that they cannot be neutral in such a situation, and have sought to defend themselves against what they clearly consider a very threatening environment. So, they have decided they must be prepared to defend themselves, and join NATO. And Putin's threats have now become reality, with his savage attack on Ukraine, confirming Europe's worst fears.

Can we still find countries which can mediate this situation? Yes, of course! There would be plenty of qualified mediators if Putin showed any willingness at all to join in peaceful discussions—peace negotiations could easily be held in, for example, Switzerland, or under UN auspices—if Russia showed any willingness at all for such a step. But without some indication by Putin that he is ready to stop the destruction and join such discussions in good faith, it is impossible to move in that direction. Unfortunately, I do not think the "neutrals" are in a position to play some sort of "in-between" role in the current world situation. Ironically, they are clearly so uneasy/afraid of what Putin is up to that they are running as fast as they can to join NATO, or any other group which might help their situation. They are all afraid of Putin's aim to bring every possible nearby country under Moscow's control! The only real "neutral" left in Europe is Switzerland, and it has a long history of maintaining that role.

Other authors claim that the beginnings stem from Molotov's proposal to the French, which was bilateral. Some European diplomats in their memoirs or interviews also argue that the Ameri-

can diplomacy was not very active, and you argued the opposite in your book. They say they were expecting the Americans to come and help out, but that the support was not there. You argue that the Americans were involved but primarily through NATO where a lot of the issues were discussed. So how do you see from your perspective the American involvement because you were the chief negotiator for most part in that period?

Well, it's true that the Americans in Washington were very skeptical about all of this. And as happens in American politics there is always a hardline contingent that warned not to get involved. They were suspicious that any kind of contact with the Russians would create openings which they would profit from. They would get into things, they would learn things. So, in the United States, but everywhere in the West as well, there were hardliners and skeptics that thought we should stay away from any contact with the Soviets, because they would only benefit from it in terms of propaganda, and they would be advertising their interest in peace, simply by having meetings. There was an enormous skepticism about having meetings with them. So, any of us who got involved in such meetings immediately were labeled "collaborationists". So, there was a strong skepticism, but the United States is a big country. There were people also in the United States who saw possibilities for doing something for easing tensions. There was no one thinking beyond easing tensions. To think beyond that was simply considered naïve. "Easing tensions" was the one area where the USA could seriously think there were possibilities and on that basis, they were prepared to go into some kind of discussions.

At the same time, within the US government, and particularly within the State Department, specifically in the section focused on Europe, and on European security, there was a strong feeling that we had to use the opportunities of any negotiating forum to seek to expand the freedoms which were available to people in Eastern Europe. We were engaged with the NATO allies in a long reflection process—which produced a NATO study called the Harmel Report (named for the Belgian Foreign Minister who led that project), that became the basis for NATO's approach to negotiations with the USSR: our negotiations were to seek (among other security-related objectives) "freer movement of people and ideas" in the USSR and Eastern Europe. That was to be the heart of our objectives, and it was a common strategy, which was to be followed by all the members of NATO, together. NATO is the place where the US leads, and all of the negotiations with the USSR were products of close coordination within NATO. Anyone who thinks the US was not active simply is ignorant of what goes on in NATO, and how this relationship works.

And at that time, NATO decided to have a single negotiator to negotiate with the Soviets – to avoid the normal divisions among the NATO member states, which were all very free and different countries! To reinforce the cohesion of the West – on the basis of the NATO group – in any negotiations which might develop, the NATO Allies decided to have a single negotiator who would represent them all, and that negotiator was to be the well-respected out-going Secretary General of the Alliance, the Italian diplomat, Manlio Brosio. He was to be what was called "the Explorer" to open negotiations with the USSR. And I was designated to be his single associate on that mission, since I was already his "Chef de Cabinet" at NATO Headquarters in Brussels. This was actually how I got my personal start in all these negotiations – I was with Brosio thru all the preparations for the negotiations at NATO in Brussels, and was designated to be his single associate when he was to open the actual negotiations with the Russians. But things did not work out that way because the Soviets refused to accept what they referred to as "a representative of a military alliance." So, the planned Brosio mission to open East-west negotiations actually never happened. Brosio retired, and instead the negotiations were started on the basis of the Soviet initiative – they asked Finland to invite all the countries of Europe and North America to meet in Helsinki, at the assembly hall called "Dipoli."

But I had been the central person in the NATO International staff tracking the Western preparations for the negotiations – quite an intense, complicated effort – so I was recruited to be the Deputy Head of the US negotiating team – when the Dipoli talks evolved into a true negotiation. This was in spite of the fact that I was in a significantly lower rank than the other members of our delegation—a unique structure but one which worked—and I "led from behind" throughout that phase of the negotiations, which is the reason why the US delegation sometimes seemed to be "low-key." But we were definitely NOT "low-key" and met regularly with the Soviet delegation to underscore Washington's engagement on the key negotiating issues—like the issue of the possibility for changes in international frontiers, which was the key issue which had to be kept open to permit (and NOT prohibit) the eventual reunification of Germany. This issue was eventually fixed with the language negotiated—personally and secretly—by Henry Kissinger with Gromyko, the famous clause on possible changes in international borders: "Frontiers can be changed, in accordance with international law, by peaceful means and by agreement." On the basis of this agreed clause—the heart of the "Helsinki Accords," Germany was subsequently reunited with no objections from any side—it had been agreed at Helsinki!—which simply validated the US-USSR agreement. Since this was the absolutely central key to East-West agreement in Helsinki, it would be pretty hard to argue—as you mention—that "the American support was not there!" Anyone who argues that simply does not know the history!

I also worked quietly, and behind the scenes, and I was an important element of the US effort during the negotiations. I worked out many, many problems through my regular (but unknown) contacts with my Soviet opposite number, who later became a senior Soviet diplomat whose career concluded with his appointment to the very influential international position as head of all UN institutions in Geneva, the biggest UN center in the world. I often saw him there, and we remained friends until he passed away. I have recounted all this in my book "Helsinki Revisited"—together he and I worked out many negotiating problems, but I have never boasted about that. My presence in those negotiations was discreet, but significant, and I was the quiet leader of the US side.

The fact that the CSCE resulted in a major historical "win" for the west was in large part due to the very discreet role which the US delegation—led in large part by myself—played. We were never out front, which obliged the Europeans to "step up," and kept the whole negotiation from becoming a US-Russian shouting match. On the contrary, we met very quietly, but regularly, with the Soviets, just to keep things under control, which permitted the Europeans to take the lead. It is their continent, and so they needed to work out their relations with the Russians! The back-bone of the West, and the reason why the Russians had to take Western positions seriously, was NATO, where the US was—and is—central. But it was not for the USA to take the lead in discussing what were largely European issues, so we deliberately stayed out of the lime-light. In this deliberate situation, my private contacts with my Soviet counterpart were essential, but remain unknown to the general public.

I think the result of this strategy speaks for itself: the Cold War ended with the whole of Eastern Europe free, Germany reunited, and a peaceful relationship between East and West in Europe celebrated at the CSCE summit in Paris. In fact, I think that in the light of Putin's efforts to unravel this peaceful situation, it would not be a bad thing to reconvene the CSCE now, to put all of Europe's pressure on Russia to push them out of Ukraine and back into their peaceful behavior of these last decades!

Just to put this into a context, can we discuss the tensions and the realities on the ground for a second? In the period when Helsinki was negotiated, many people did not have basic human rights despite the UN Charter already being adopted. Some people were not able to leave their country and would be shot at the border which had a barbed wire. There were political prosecutions. The universal human rights did not apply to all the people. Then Helsinki was negotiated and something miraculous happened. The dissident movements in Czechoslovakia and Poland grew and with them the expectation that the people will enjoy the freedoms signed in Helsinki. They expected reforms in their countries and in the national legislation. Charter

77 says that from Helsinki the "citizens have the right, and our state the duty, to abide by them". Why was Helsinki so powerful?

With respect to the growing hope among the dissidents, I think they would have jumped on anything that we produced, because it was bound to be softer than the regular line of the Communist governments. But I think it was something more than that. In some cases there were some real commitments that were considered quite advantageous, like family reunification. There were a few other things that were significant at the time. So, it wasn't just nothing at the end. But I think that anything that came out of there would have been used as a tool by the dissidents, the people who were interested in this. We saw that immediately after Helsinki was signed. In my book ("Helsinki Revisited") I cite the story of a female taxi driver in New York. She was part of a very small number of Jews who were permitted by the Soviets to emigrate at that time because of the Helsinki Agreement. After Helsinki was signed, they knew that they would have to show something, and they chose to release some Jewish immigrants, and that woman, a taxi driver I had in New York, was one of those. So, there were some symbolic things that were done, enough so that the people who are interested in these problems were able to point to them and say that there was something that we got from this agreement. I think it was enough to convince people that there were possibilities there. And that is what encouraged the dissidents throughout the eastern part of Europe. It inspired them to think that they can get more and by pushing they were able to get more. That was just the beginning. It was like the story of the tiny hole in the dike, with just a tiny flow of water, which simply grew and grew as people learned that there were new commitments on freer travel, and families decided to take advantage of them. Of course, there was also a broadly-based fear that the opportunity to travel more freely might not last very long, so many people decided to leave quickly, to leave immediately — and simply drove to the nearest border and walked across — (sounds familiar). I have told the story often of the huge wave of East Germans who started crossing the border from Hungary into Austria when they learned that the Hungarian government had eased their restrictions on that border. Whole families of East Germans simply abandoned their tiny East German "Trabant" cars along the side of the road, and hitchhiked across the border into Austria, where they went as fast as they could to the West German embassy in Vienna. I used to pass that embassy on my way to my office in central Vienna, where we were still negotiating, and there was a line of refugees along the street and around the corner, waiting their turn. They all knew that under West German law any German had the right to a West German passport. So, these refugees from East Germany entered the Embassy as East Germans and came out as West Germans! They were transformed. And this was at least partly because of the impact of our negotiations. It was truly a transformative moment in Europe.

I used to travel across that frontier, between East and West, from time to time, and I knew it pretty well. It was a chilling experience because the landscape was increasingly barren as one approached the border crossing. There were no cars at all, because people could not travel. I was an exception because—as an American diplomat—it was easy for me to get visas and to travel anywhere. In fact, I went to Prague with my family several times. The streets in Prague were empty—even the lively narrow streets near the river—there were no crowds of tourists then, as there are now. I recall one day when I was there with my family—just as tourists—we looked for a place to have lunch, and literally could not find one in the center of Prague. There were no restaurants—everything was bleak and ominous. Later I lived in Prague, after the Cold War was over—up on the hill on that narrow street which goes down to the Castle. I was the President of the private organization which took over the functions of Radio Free Europe and Radio Liberty, and their associated publications. My office was in the one "sky-scraper" which existed in Prague at that time. Each morning I would walk down the long narrow streets from the hill to take the underground metro to my office. And it was always filled with people, filled with life—music and shops and cafes! And I would reflect on those extraordinary changes—

Prague was transformed into such a colorful, interesting place—a place one never wanted to leave!

All that was, I believe, largely due to the way "Helsinki" — the idea of "Helsinki" — inspired ordinary people in all of what we called—at that time—Eastern Europe. They were inspired by the "Helsinki accords" to press and insist on their rights, their freedoms, and it changed many things. It changed everything! Within a few years Eastern Europe was transformed. I watched it happen. I was there. Those crowds of ordinary people, in Prague, and in Poland, and in East Germany—all over the East—were inspired by our work on the so-called "Helsinki Accords." That is the key thing about freedom—it inspires people, brings out the best and most creative elements in them. Those who have never experienced it do not always understand this phenomenon—free people become creative people, thinking people—and it changes everything.

That was what you call "Helsinki's power"—the power of this idea of freedom, which had been so repressed in Eastern Europe! And now Moscow, and Putin, are trying to take that away from Russia's nearest neighbor, Ukraine—in total violation of the Helsinki Accords—and every international norm. He is trying to reverse history, and to take that freedom away from Russia's nearest neighbor, in a spectacular violation of—not only Helsinki, but of all the norms of international relations! It is a colossal, mind-boggling violation, so spectacular that it took some time for many people in the West to realize what was going on! We worked long and hard to bring the norms of freedom to Eastern Europe and the USSR, and we cannot now permit them to be swept away by this Putin!

As you know, I was sent as a special American Ambassador to open US relations with each of the "newly independent States," following the break-up of the USSR, and Kiev was the first place I visited on that unique mission, so I know the region pretty well.

Ukraine, like all the states which composed the USSR, is a naturally-independent country, with its own national identity. It is not somehow a possession of Russia! This is why we must all join to prevent that! We cannot go back to the period of Cold War, when parts of Europe were deprived of their natural human freedoms. We gained those freedoms through long, hard negotiations, without firing a shot. They are the natural rights of all Europeans, all human beings. They are the natural rights of Ukrainians — and also of Russians, by the way! We all know how valuable these rights are, for everyone, and we cannot allow them to be taken away on Putin's whim. This is where we must take our stand, with Ukraine. They are fighting for the same rights we sought in the Helsinki negotiations, and we must stand with them. There is no question about it. It is our fight, every bit as much as it is theirs.

There was another new thing that happened. The first follow-up meeting. It was in 1977 in Belgrade and for the first time, governments were reporting on human rights violations in other countries. This was the first time we were looking into what others are doing, and that is remembered in the history of the OSCE as a turning point, a harsh moment that was not well accepted by the Soviets. It turned into reporting violations of what was agreed in Helsinki.

The Soviets were thinking they would sign this document and gradually people would forget about it. But that is not how it was seen by the West, especially by people who were engaged on these issues. Lobbyists, for example, in Washington became very active immediately on the basis of these very minor commitments and they used them in ways the Soviets did not anticipate. They were the foot in the door and we had gotten our foot in the door. Then you had all kinds of groups that tried to build on that. It is true that if you took one of these ideas, like for instance family reunification, it could be very small, or it could be very big. It depends on how you interpreted the language, and how many people applied, and a lot of things that were not really controllable. I think the Soviets could not have anticipated the effects of all this. They did not have the same experience with lobbying groups as we had in the West. We knew that any one of these ideas would be like ammunition for these lobbying groups, and they would push on these things in the United States, but throughout Europe as well,

because we were used to that. But they didn't have that same experience in Russia and I think they never dreamed of the kind of
reaction and activities that would blossom from these modest
commitments that they had made. They somehow thought you
make a tiny commitment and that means a tiny result, a tiny con-
cession, and a tiny effect. But no, a tiny commitment can sometimes have a huge effect. That was the difference.

For many years — before and after the Helsinki negotiations —
there was an ongoing debate in Washington about whether it was
more advantageous to try to handle delicate matters with the
USSR privately or publicly. The same sort of debate comes up pe-
riodically with respect to other sensitive international issues.
There were solid arguments on both sides — by handling an issue
privately, it may be possible to find a private, but satisfactory, solution, while handling an issue publicly is always risky — it can
create pressures for the other side to be more forthcoming, or it
can close the matter completely and render any solution impossible. There have been good examples on both sides of this debate.
When Jimmy Carter was elected President, those favoring "public
diplomacy" on human rights issues came into the Administration
and so this became an official Washington strategy, replacing the
secrecy and back-channeled "private diplomacy" used by Kissinger under Presidents Nixon and Ford. The changes which took
place in the US strategy for the CSCE review meeting in Belgrade
reflected a broader change from private to public handling of
CSCE issues, resulting from the change in the White House. President's Jimmy Carter's appointment of former Supreme Court Justice Arthur Goldberg to be the Head of the US Delegation in Belgrade reflected Carter's intention to use the CSCE as a highly pro-
vocative public lever for his active human rights advocacy concerning the USSR and Eastern Europe. This was a very sharp
change of general policy from the Kissinger years. Ambassador
Bud Sherer was retained as Goldberg's Deputy, but Goldberg
completely overshadowed him, and made human rights in the
Communist countries into a banner public policy of the US Administration. With Goldberg as the leader of the US Delegation the
famous US "low profile" in the CSCE was a thing of the past, and

the Belgrade meeting became very contentious as he raised specific names and cases, and did not hesitate to address issues publicly.

The Soviet negotiators did not consider the Helsinki Final Act to be a bad deal for them. They couldn't envisage the aftermath and could not predict the events between 1977-1990. Could you? Was this something that the Western diplomats were hoping for or it was a surprise to you as well?

Of course no one could foresee what would happen after the Helsinki Final Act was signed—but we knew what our objectives were, which we had stipulated in our proposals, and which became new international obligations for the signatory countries when the Final Act was signed. I went back to Washington as the Head of the State Department office that was responsible for implementation of what had been agreed in the Final Act. And that instantly became a huge bureaucratic challenge. All the lobbying groups in Washington were inspired by the new commitments which were contained in the Final Act. These activists saw them as being much more significant than the way we were interpreting them as bureaucrats, and began pushing for immediate implementation of those commitments by the Soviet Union and the Eastern European countries. They wanted immediate, concrete action! And the first thing I had to do was very unusual in those days—I had to buy a computer! At that time, no one in Washington even knew what a "computer" was!

In my small office, which was responsible for pursuing the implementation of what had been agreed in the Helsinki Final Act, we started receiving mountains of information—reports, complaints, etc.—about individual human rights cases, all over Eastern Europe and the Soviet Union. There were so many individual cases that just tracking them became almost impossible. Then somebody told me I'd better get a computer. I said, "What's a computer?" Computers simply didn't exist at that time. So, I looked into this, and discovered that we could buy this thing called a computer which would track information on a machine.

So, I ordered one and it was delivered to my section's offices — it was the very first computer in the US State Department! It looked like a big, old-fashioned steamer trunk with four legs, and I had it installed against the wall. It had various things that you operated — switches and dials — to make use of it to track information. It was a plain computer, and it was the very first computer in the State Department. The first thing we had to do was to figure out how to use it, which we did, and it quickly became indispensable because we had mountains of letters and reports on incidents which related to the obligations contained in the Helsinki Final Act — all of which had to be recorded, summarized, and tabulated by country and type of incident, because this was to become the record of the "implementation" of the human rights provisions of the Helsinki Final Act.

I immediately had to increase the size of the office, because there was so much stuff to do — just recording, grouping, summarizing and constantly updating this material took a lot of time, and I added staff to our office to track it all. People were sending in letters — someone had a cousin in Prague, or a friend in Moscow, or there was a news report from somewhere. Some people managed to get out of the Soviet Union, but left their children behind and wrote to us asking for help for their family to get back together — on the basis of the "family reunification" provisions of the Helsinki Final Act. All of these appeals for help were based on the commitments contained in the Helsinki Final Act, but many required approaches to the government in Moscow, so that we had to find the best way to raise the issue with the Russians. And every individual story was different, requiring research, verification, and judgement before the US government could become involved. And everything had to be recorded, tabulated, and tracked on our computer — so everybody in my office staff had to learn what a computer was. That's why this early version of a computer was so big — they were still experimenting — long before the laptop versions came out.

My small office was immediately overwhelmed, trying to keep up with all this record-keeping and decision-making on individual cases. And not only that, but in Congress they picked this up and were running all over the place with it—every Congressman wanted to use these new international commitments for the benefit of their constituents, and the constituents inevitably included, for example, families that had emigrated but who had left behind their sisters or their cousins, and wanted to ensure that they, too, could leave the USSR.

So this whole operation—the "implementation of the provisions of the Helsinki Final Act"—became a real cutting-edge activity in Washington, because many people, all across the country, went directly to their congressmen or senators to seek help with some specific thing, and each case was different, had to be decided on its own merits, etc. And this was not just for the USSR—it was relevant for all the countries of Eastern Europe, which were all governed at that time by Communist governments, whose practices were similar to those of the USSR. And of course when relatives who were constituents raised such heart-rending family issues with their senators and congressmen the senators and congressmen immediately raised these matters with us, and it all came to my office, where we added personnel but had a difficult time even keeping up with the rapidly-growing surge of individual cases.

To make matters more complicated, a few Congressmen started complaining that we were not handling these cases fast enough, or as actively as we should. A bill was passed creating what came to be called "The Helsinki Commission," a new joint Congressional-Administration committee focusing exclusively on the commitments of the Helsinki Final Act. At a certain point, the newly-inaugurated president, Jimmy Carter, who had no previous experience in Washington, sent a handwritten note to Cyrus Vance, his Secretary of State. The note read as follows—literally: "Who is this guy Maresca, who is screwing up our relations with Congress?" Just handwritten on a small piece of paper, which was then hand-carried by courier from the White House to the State Department to be delivered to the Secretary of State. So, I was really on the edge of disaster when that happened. Fortunately, the Secretary of State, Cyrus Vance, was a very rational person. Not only that, he was an alumnus and the chairman of the Board of

Trustees of the school that I had also gone to—Kent School—so he knew my name. I was one of the very few people from that school who was in the Foreign Service, working in the State Department. Maybe there were two of us from the Kent School in the whole Foreign Service, and Vance was a trustee of that school. So, when he read Carter's note, and saw my name, of course he made the connection and knew exactly who I was in this note from the President.

The reason Carter had complained was that some Congressman had gone to him and complained that Congress was not getting full cooperation on getting people out of the Soviet Union and the guy who is responsible for this hold-up was some guy named Maresca. Vance surely didn't even know that we were tabulating all of this stuff on our big computer in the building there below him, but he was the Secretary of State. Of course he could not know everything that was going on in the Department he had just taken charge of. So right away I was put in jeopardy by that complaint—it is pretty unusual for a junior official in the State Department to be the subject of a personal complaint to the President! My friends said: "it's better for you to move to some other position." I DID NOT move to another position—I was always pretty determined to do my job—but that was what life was like. We were all running to keep up with the requirements of following up on all of these very specific family cases, on the basis of the commitments of the Helsinki Final Act.

Of course, the Final Act was an achievement in itself—a history-changing achievement, as we can now see—but it required an almost infinite amount of "follow-up," which entailed making presentations on individual human rights cases at the foreign ministries of communist countries, etc. The commitments contained in the Final Act had to be made known, individual cases had to be identified, compared with the specific commitments, etc. before they could be raised, and that was an enormous "follow-up" challenge. But it was undertaken, carefully and slowly, by all the West European countries which had individual "cases" of concern to them—typically of Russian emigre families with relatives who were still in the USSR or Eastern Europe. This became a huge new diplomatic effort, all across Europe and North America, and it went on for years. In fact, there are still many individual human rights cases being discussed on the basis of the "Helsinki Commitments." And it was these commitments which finally undermined the whole structure of the Communist regimes in Eastern Europe, and stimulated the break-up of the Soviet hold over those countries, and eventually of the Soviet Union itself.

It is interesting you are mentioning the way requests to government went through lobbyists. The pressure must have been very big that it would make the State Department do the kind of work that you were doing, simply because there were requests from constituencies.

But that was always the case. Lobbyists required a lot of handling. You have to try to do something, even if they ask for something that is totally impossible. Very often lobbyists will be demanding something that's totally impossible, and everybody in the State Department knows that it's totally impossible, but when new people come in, like Jimmy Carter, for example, who had no experience in foreign policy at all, they didn't know that there were millions of people being held as hostages essentially, and were not permitted to emigrate. That was a very long-standing problem and you could not just resolve it overnight.

The lobbyists had no role during the negotiations themselves—they did not know what was going on, and had no basis for pressuring the government in Washington until the final agreement had been reached. At that point they could pressure the US government to insist that the commitments in the Final Act had to be carried out, and to press the USSR and the other Communist countries to respect their commitments with respect to what was called "the freer movement of people and ideas" throughout Europe. There were concrete commitments which had to be carried out, and Congress immediately started pressing the State Department to insist that they were fully carried out and respected. This was of course very difficult to do. We could not impose concrete punishments for specific failures, and most of the commitments in the Helsinki Final Act were very general, so even the way they were carried out was open to discussion and disagreement. But we did indeed start checking individual cases in which human rights had not been respected. The problem was that this is a monumental task! There were thousands of individual cases, in all the countries which were under Communist governments at that time—throughout Eastern Europe, as well as throughout the USSR, which was huge and was largely unknown to the West. Each case was different, and not all of them were even known! Just imagine: each individual case had to become known, the facts checked, and then a Western government had to take the political decision to focus on that specific case. Normally a government will only do that if it has an obvious national interest in the case—such as family members who are citizens of that Western country, so that it may be a question of family reunification. Each case must be considered on its specific facts before a government has an obvious national interest in that specific case. And there were thousands of such cases—each one of which had complex aspects which had to be taken into account. Governments do not enter such cases without full confidence that they have a legitimate interest. So, it was a massive undertaking and it took some time just to arrange the bureaucracy to be able to manage what was a huge new workload, requiring expertise, reporting from distant (and very closed) societies. I moved as fast as possible to set up and arrange such a capacity in the State Department, but it was a whole new apparatus and took some time. And of course, there were many people who expected results immediately, and while the effects of the Helsinki agreements were, over time, tangible and positive, it obviously did not, and could not possibly, happen overnight. I was invited to speak to a group of professors at the Harvard Faculty Club at one point, and everyone complained that they "had not been kept informed" of developments during the negotiations, and I responded that it was not our responsibility as diplomats to keep professors informed. And there was skepticism about the possible results, to which I responded by recounting one case—just one of many cases—where children had been reunited with their parents on the basis of the "Helsinki" commitments. I said that if just one child was reunited with his or her parents, then our work was worth the effort.

This is an element of democracy though, right? Lobbyists represent certain groups of the demos and in the Charter of Paris that connection is strengthened and reaffirmed. It became an expectation that in all countries of the CSCE, later OSCE "democratic government is based on the will of the people, expressed regularly through free and fair elections" and that "democracy, with its representative and pluralist character, entails accountability to the electorate, the obligation of public authorities to comply with the law and justice administered impartially." Is what you are describing the responsibility felt by the government towards the demos?

When you read the language in these documents, or some of these commitments, it is pretty impressive, and we owe that to the neutrals. We went into that negotiation on the HFA, especially on the principles, with very formal language, which, of course, the Soviets at that time just rejected and they didn't want to have such a list. They didn't want to have text at all and it took a long time for them to accept that you would have more than just the names of those principles. They would have been satisfied with that. That's what the Soviets wanted. Just a list of names like "non-intervention in internal affairs". Instead, what they got is four paragraphs on what that means. But to have those sentences added – it took two years. Those things were not settled until the last days. On the very last days, I think, maybe two or three days before we actually concluded the negotiations, we had maybe ten problems that remained on which there was no agreement, even in those principles. I called up Dubinin and I said: "We got to solve these problems". He said: "Yes, I agree with you. How are we going to do that? "And I said: "Meet me in front of the fireplace". There was a delegate's lounge and it was very nice, a very cozy kind of place with comfortable chairs. I went up there with an interpreter and a couple of experts, because I didn't know every history of every problem that remained in these texts. But I had pieces of paper marking every place where we had a problem, and I started –

page one—here is a problem. We went through one by one, and we solved each of those problems one by one. I was there for three hours with him and he was the worst person you ever wanted to deal with. He was such a nasty guy. He wouldn't let anything pass without making it into a nasty confrontation. Instinctively, he was one of the worst human beings I've ever known in my life and he was the last person in the world that you had any kind of feeling to be reasonable with. But we had to get through it. The date had already been fixed for the signature, and we still had these open issues. We spent several hours there and we solved them all. The distance between the positions was so huge, and it was only because at that point Dubinin also felt pressure to finish, because the date had already been set and they were going to Helsinki, just like we were going. That's the only reason he accepted some of these things.

What was the road from Helsinki to Paris? Many things happened in between...

The Europeans wanted to take account of the changes that were happening, to prepare a new Summit-level gathering, to reflect the significance of the historical moment we were seeing taking form and to lay the basis for peaceful relations in Europe. Phrases like "a common European home" and "creation of a peaceful order in Europe", were used to describe the objectives of such a meeting. The Soviet President, Mikhail Gorbachev, proposed such a meeting to President Francois Mitterrand in Kyiv in December 1989 and Mitterrand immediately supported this idea. There was recognition that events were moving swiftly, that the entire European balance was changing the possibility of German reunification, so it became clear that measures were needed to ensure that the coming evolution would happen peacefully. So, the CSCE was re-convened using the format of delegations accredited to the CSBM (Confidence and Security Building Measures) negotiations, to prepare for a new CSCE Summit, to take place in Paris, which jumped up the importance of our negotiations—in terms of the world stage—in a way that had never happened before.

It was also a shift in who "owned" the CSCE. Up until that time the CSCE was "owned" by the Soviet Union. It was their initiative; it was their idea. The Russians secretly got the Finns to offer an invitation. That was kept secret for years, but gradually people came to know. The Finns were very sensitive about this, because they do not like to be portrayed as being manipulatable, especially by the Soviets. But that was the way it happened. That was the reason why the Finns invited the European countries, plus the US and Canada, to Dipoli for the first meetings.

I think the Summit in Paris upgraded the image of the CSCE as an institution in ways that are hard to qualify, because Paris is such a center—for the press, for public attention. Everybody knows that things that happen in Paris are by definition important. So, it changed the whole order of magnitude. The optics were also very important. I think that was a great gesture by Mitterrand and he benefited from it, just like any other politician would.

Was Paris a way to formalize the dialogue that was informally happening before, from Dipoli through Geneva and the follow up meetings (Belgrade, Madrid and Vienna)?

I think CSCE's peak was probably that meeting in Paris, and unfortunately for the CSCE, there are a lot of other things that now have taken place. The CSCE had its day and was important at the time, but is not relevant now. If someone tomorrow proposes a new summit-level session of the OSCE to resolve the problem of Ukraine then maybe suddenly it will take center stage again. But nobody is doing that. It is kind of hard to imagine—where would it be, to begin with? It would have to be somewhere in the middle to symbolically fit that role and who would do it? Would the Turks do it for example? Would they offer to do it in Istanbul? Without some new lift off like that the OSCE is irrelevant today. The issues are different now and the dangers are more present.

The CSCE institutions have never been able to acquire the strength, nor the influence, which we optimistically thought they might acquire, and when the break-up of the USSR left Gorbachev without any official position, Russia began its long return to the harsh, dictatorial government which was the tradition there. That made it impossible for the CSCE institutions to have any impact, and they did not really survive in any meaningful way. Maybe the time will come when they can be revived, but sadly I do not see that happening in the current circumstances.

In the early days of the CSCE one of the factors, which was always a consideration when we started thinking about how things would go in such a body, was how close we were at any given moment to actual combat, to having a war. And I think history has shown that you can only get to the kind of discussions that we have had in the CSCE over time if you are relatively far away from having an actual war. Whereas right now we're not only close to having a war, we are having a war. There has been an incredible amount of destruction and mindless, deliberate cruelty and the dangers of wider, more destructive war, are more present than ever before. Perhaps we are in circumstances where people start to think in terms of some kind of device that could be used to bring us back to reason, but I don't think Putin cares about anything like that anymore and probably Western leaders do not think Putin should be saved by giving him a way out. So, the idea of having some kind of dialogue in the midst of killing people is very remote, but maybe that time will come. Maybe — if there were to be some kind of a practical settlement of the war, and the destruction, the killings of people, even children, were to fade into history, tensions were to be eased over time — and Putin himself were to disappear — it might be possible to get back to a situation where you could have more of a dialogue and all the things that the CSCE can do might become relevant. But we are certainly not there now, and whether we will ever get back to that kind of stage is an open issue.

The Charter of Paris is known as the most enthusiastic document, some even call it a poetry in the international law. Did you have a feeling it was a consequence of the enthusiasm built by the rapprochement, the reunification of Germany and by the fall of the iron curtain? Was this spirit captured? Were there,

though, early warnings that were sidelined by the "good news"? The dissolutions that happened very soon after Paris (USSR and Czechoslovakia) and the war in Yugoslavia were a sign that we were not equipped for managing conflicts within the state, ethnic conflicts and identity issues.

There were certainly many signs that warned of what was to come—that the warm and friendly atmosphere of the Summit meeting in Paris was "too good to last." But in many ways that warmth was a genuine reflection of the fact that the likelihood of a major world war seemed to have been greatly diminished by Gorbachev, by the liberalization he had encouraged in Russia, and by the positive atmosphere of our negotiations in the CSCE. But as we now know, that positive atmosphere did not last very long, and soon there were indications of serious difficulties to come.

Perhaps the most concrete signal during that period that everything was not in perfect order was Gorbachev's personal reaction when he learned that the leaders of the three Baltic States were attending the Paris summit meeting of the CSCE! Of course they were only in the outer corridors of the meeting hall—as observers, under a special arrangement I had personally worked out with my counterpart, the Russian Ambassador to our negotiations, and the informal group of countries which supported the independence of The Baltic States—mainly the USA and the Scandinavian countries. I happened to be standing near Gorbachev, who was talking to President Bush in the lobby of the conference, during a coffee break, when he saw the Baltic State representatives across the entrance lobby of the building. They had been admitted—only to the outer corridors—on a special arrangement reflecting the fact that a number of the participating states, including the US (which meant me, as the head of the US delegation), had always recognized their independence. We reached a compromise with the Soviet delegation under which the representatives of The Baltic States could circulate in the outer corridors of the huge meeting hall we were using in Paris. So, the Baltic State representatives, with their own entry badges, were circulating in these outer corridors, and they were very well-known figures in Russia because they were actively holding demonstrations and agitating for their independence. And Gorbachev actually saw them during a coffee break, and recognized their leaders, and it seems that he had not been told by his diplomats that they had agreed to an arrangement under which these well-known "dissidents" would be present in the "outer corridors" of the Paris meeting!

So, there was a brief "diplomatic incident" when Gorbachev saw The Baltic States representatives in the corridor outside the grand meeting hall where the speeches were going on, and recognized them! He immediately protested to Mitterrand, who called his security chief over and whispered something to him, actually covering his mouth with his hand! And the French security agents immediately, but very politely, escorted the Baltic State representatives from the building. I rushed across the great entrance hall to inform President Bush and Secretary of State Baker of what was happening, which was all I could do—the CSCE operated on the basis of consensus, so a single objection to the presence of the Baltic State representatives meant they could not attend. I had personally checked with my Soviet counterpart, the Ambassador who was the head of the Soviet delegation, to ensure that the Soviets would not object to the presence of the Baltic State Representatives in the outer corridors of the Summit meeting in Paris, and he had just shrugged and had not raised an objection. But obviously Gorbachev had not been informed! And for an instant Gorbachev was visibly very angry! But Mitterrand then helped, and engaged him in a positive discussion, and very soon the two of them were smiling and nodding their heads. And then Mitterrand, who I knew quite well from my days as the US Minister in Paris, gave me a nod to say "everything was okay." That incident was certainly a setback at that moment—for those of us who were pressing for the independence of The Baltic States. As you may know, the USA continued to have embassies representing the three independent Baltic states in Washington, throughout their "forced incorporation" into the USSR, and during the CSCE negotiations I personally developed an informal "Friends of The Baltic States" group within the CSCE, to do what we could to involve the Baltic state representatives, to keep them informed, and to support their lobbying efforts for their independence. And later, within a few months after the Paris Summit, Moscow actually accepted the independence of the three Baltic States! I have studied the way the Baltic peoples pressed for their independence during that period, when they began asserting their right to independence increasingly loudly — in newspapers and on the radio — and I believe this small incident in Paris was a true milestone for them: within a few months after the Paris meeting, Moscow actually recognized their independence. After all our small group of "Friends of The Baltic States," meeting "on the fringes of the negotiation," had some effect, and very shortly after the Paris summit, they were free!

I focused a lot on some lesser-known issues during that last period of my role in the CSCE, including one very specific conflict — the one over Nagorno Karabakh. At a certain point I became a kind-of "engine" for trying to find a solution to that issue — which I ultimately concluded was totally impossible at the time. And that was the issue on which I decided to leave the diplomatic profession. I "broke my sword" on that very issue, as they say. It still is unresolved, and won't be resolved in our lifetimes, if ever. There are many situations like that one around the former Soviet Union, and we don't even know of some of these. The Russians, of course, do, and I have to give them some credit here, because these are situations that they have been dealing with for a couple hundred years or more. In some cases, they've added to the problems, that's for sure. Nagorno Karabakh is one of those places where they've added to the problems. But there is no question that the region which was the Soviet Union contains many, barely covered up, bloody rivalries, ancient rivalries, which the Russians have dealt with over many years and centuries. Those are Russian troops up there in the mountains of Karabakh, between the Armenians and the Azeris, doing the same thing. Of course, it's in their interest, in a way, because that's the way they keep control over the whole region. Nonetheless, you have to give them credit for dealing with these awful, bloody conflicts, which no other world power wants to get involved in.

The case of Nagorno Karabakh is an example of how some of these "ethnic conflicts" came into existence, or were prolonged by history. The story dates from the time when the newly-constituted Soviet Union sent a commission around its far-flung lands, to review and establish the new boundaries among the many "Socialist Republics" that formed the USSR. The commission was chaired by Joseph Stalin himself, who was, at that time, still a rising Party official. In each country this commission held open "hearings" to hear arguments about the proposed boundaries of each Republic. In each case the commission would listen to the various positions on the proposed boundaries, then they would discuss these matters in closed meetings, and the next day they would announce the approved boundaries. These decisions inevitably left some local groups unhappy!

This happened also in Azerbaijan, and then in Armenia, with discussions focusing on the boundary line between the two states. During the hearings some participants argued that the region of Nagorno Karabakh was populated largely by ethnic Armenians, and should therefore be included in the new state of Armenia, but that under the boundaries which had been proposed, that region would fall within Azerbaijan, not Armenia. The commission listened to all the arguments, and then went into closed session to discuss the matter. The following morning the meeting was open, and the Commission announced its conclusions, including the boundary line which would be approved between the two countries. The announced boundary was exactly what it is today, with Nagorno Karabakh (largely populated by Armenians) falling within the boundaries of Azerbaijan. And those boundaries are still the official boundaries today. No one knows what the discussions of the commission—which were behind closed doors and were not recorded—addressed, or why this anomaly was left as it was. And the inclusion of Armenian-dominated Nagorno Karabakh within Azerbaijan has been a key problem in the war which has gone on in that region for twenty years or more.

The issue of such "ethnic" conflicts came up in the negotiations of the documents that were produced in Paris, and as I recall the overall conclusion was that it was just too difficult for outsiders to deal with issues like that. Nobody really came out and said that, but the general reaction was that these conflicts are so diffi-

cult that we will have to "kick the ball down the road a bit," before really confronting the issue. And so, this issue, and other such
issues, have been left aside; they are considered "too difficult".
Unlike the Helsinki CSCE document, the Paris document was giv-
en a very short preparation time, something like two or three
months. In the preparation of Helsinki, we spent a few years in
very difficult negotiations and had to leave some issues out because even with a couple of years to negotiate these issues are still
out there! And in many of these situations, like the one in Nagorno Karabakh, nobody seems to have an idea of what might be a
true solution. There are no thoughts, no formulas, out there for
reaching some kind of solution. Nagorno Karabakh is not the only
place like that. Former Yugoslavia was also like that. Filled with
places that had a mix of the many nationalities that composed
what was Yugoslavia, and many of these places were filled with
hatred and old rivalries, where it is very difficult to find peace.

**How can we then manage diversity in society differently? Or do
we have to end into polarization that then becomes a violent
conflict, and then leads to dissolution? Was it possible to prevent the escalations in Paris already maybe?**

The simple answer is no. I've been wrestling with this challenge of
hatreds between national groupings, ever since I got into the
CSCE subjects. And even before that, because growing up in the
United States, you run into this all the time. I ran into this myself
when I was growing up with an Italian name. That may sound
remote to nowadays because Italian names are now accepted more
widely. But having an Italian name when I was growing up was
very much like having some more exotic kind of name now. Italians who had emigrated to the United States were very poor people from the lower classes in Italy. Those were obviously the ones
who wanted to leave. If you were rich and living in Italy, you
would live very nicely. Many of these people were illiterate. I was
born in Italy, with an Italian father, but my mother was American—she had won a fellowship to study painting in Italy, and had
married my father there. So, my mother was American, and my

sister and I were both Italian and American. We lived a very privileged life, on the shore of Lago Maggiore, near the Swiss border. My mother only left Italy to take her two small children to safety in America when war broke out in Europe, but my father was not allowed to leave—Italian males could not leave because of the war. And we were not immigrants to the USA; my mother was from St. Louis, and her two children were born Americans. But the US has always received huge numbers of immigrants, including many Italians, and as a diplomat I became interested in this general subject, which has now become a central world problem, a challenge for every country. So, if we were organizing the agenda for a European conference now, we would surely include immigration, or "migration" as a general subject, because it is looming as one of the great challenges of our time. This, I think, is a key subject, which has become very timely and central, in both Europe and North America—a discussion of migration, of immigration and of racial differences within European and North American societies, because every society in Europe and North America is now faced with exactly the same issues. That was not true twenty years ago, probably not even ten years ago. It was just budding ten years ago, but now it's so squarely in the foreground in practically all the countries of Europe, because of immigration. And they're faced with more problems because the immigration is going to grow. Everybody is scared of it, but inevitably it's going to grow.

Back to the OSCE. In Paris for the first time some sort of basic structure was created. A big milestone. In later documents that structure was upgraded. Do you think that we are here now as a consequence of not upgrading sufficiently or not living up to the prescriptions or because we are behind the developments on the ground? How do we protect multilateralism from such big shocks? What does resilience mean if our structures are fragile even when based on commitments and so many negotiated concepts. Having the Charter of Paris and its beautifully written pledges for us to live in peace and prosperity should have prevented February 2022. How do we do that this time around?

What would your recommendation be to build-in resilience into the machinery?

The CSCE summit in Paris produced some very important agreements — at least they would have been important, historically, if they had been respected and maintained. But they were not. They were deliberately and spectacularly broken by Vladimir Putin with his invasion of Ukraine. That event was the culmination of a long series of events in Russia which have been aimed at reversing the dissolution of the USSR that was carried out by Boris Yeltsin when he withdrew Russia from the USSR, which had the immediate effect of ending the existence of the USSR, and thus deliberately ended the career of Mikhail Gorbachev, who was the President of the USSR. That action was deliberately planned and carried out by Yeltsin, in cooperation with the KGB, in order to terminate Gorbachev's political career, because he was simply considered too "Western-leaning" for the hardline traditionalists in Moscow. It was nothing less than a back-room coup d'état. Gorbachev, whose only official position was as President of the USSR, was left without a job, and was sidelined, which was the objective the maneuver. And Vladimir Putin was introduced to the public as the planned successor to Yeltsin, who would carry out the long-term reconstruction of the full USSR.

All of this has played out over the years, before our eyes, but there was an important and unforeseen problem which arose before the USSR could be fully re-assembled: the population of Ukraine resisted being absorbed again into what had been the USSR. Ukraine, under the popularly-elected leadership of Volodimir Zelensky, clearly wanted to maintain its independence, and resisted being brought back under Moscow's control. And Russia then invaded Ukraine to enforce Putin's vision of a reunited USSR. The relations established by the Charter of Paris, and the structures set up at that time, are totally meaningless as long as there is a vicious and aggressive leadership in the Kremlin which is trying to subjugate a neighboring state thru a vicious war!

So, we are now far beyond the commitments of the Charter of Paris, and I think the utility of that agreement may well have been completely destroyed. Certainly, as long as Russia continues to be run by Putin, or someone like him, as a dictatorial regime with the clear objective of re-establishing Moscow's control over the whole of what was the USSR, there will be no possibility of peaceful relations with Europe and North America. Absolutely zero possibility! Putin will have to disappear, and Russia will have to make major efforts to be recognized as a peaceful, democratic country, before any kind of confidence can be restored. The Charter of Paris has no meaning in the current situation, and we will probably have to get to a new sort of "Charter," and certainly a new government in Moscow, before there can be any hope for normal international relations with Russia.

This makes the work of any international forum very difficult, not just the OSCE. The invasion of Ukraine will have long-term consequence for the UN system as well. Will it be possible to reconcile the diverging narratives after Russia invaded Ukraine and has waged a very destructive war or will this require rethinking the whole international order?

The UN structure is antique. If there were any sensible approach to these things — which there isn't, because it's all politicized — one would update the whole structure and the way it operates, so that everything could be upgraded and modernized. But that won't happen because some countries will resist changes that might reduce their independence.

In addition, we face a whole new international context following Putin's open aggression on Ukraine. That has signaled a willingness to carry out extraordinary, completely uncalled-for violence in pursuit of the conquest of a neighboring sovereign state, which the world has not seen since Hitler's time. This raises the "Putin problem" to one of world-wide consequence and urgency. The UN simply cannot deal with such a problem, because the country which has created this problem has a veto power in the UN!

So, unfortunately the world — especially the NATO allies and our friends in other parts of the world — will have to go back to the basics of international relations, and start a process of isolating Russia and Putin, perhaps for a very long time, in a kind of "New Cold War." The objectives of this isolation should be to encourage Russia to change course, to end its use of violence to enforce its will on its neighbors, and to seek acceptance by the World Community. Countries which support the Russian position in this situation will have to be subjected to the same isolation as is imposed on Russia. This type of approach is not very effective, but it is the best way of responding to unacceptable behavior without actually starting a war.

Over the longer term I think we need to consider ways to encourage more normal international behavior by Russia, and to impose really meaningful sanctions when a country discards so completely the norms of peaceful international relations. As difficult as it may be, we need to construct an international system which can enforce the rules of peaceful international behavior. Experience over time has shown how difficult it is to obtain meaningful international commitments which cannot simply be ignored when a country decides to do that.

After the break-up of the USSR, you were asked by Secretary of State, Baker to carry out a unique assignment — to go on a special, year-long assignment, to officially open direct US diplomatic relations with each of the "newly-independent states from the former USSR". Was that the first occasion on which a US Ambassador was sent directly to open diplomatic relations with Ukraine? What were the highlights, new realizations or some stories you would like to share from this historic assignment?

Yes, it was. Of course, other US Ambassadors had visited Ukraine many times, while it was a part of the Soviet Union, but none had gone there as a US Ambassador on an official visit to the independent state of Ukraine. I was sent on this mission to open direct US diplomatic relations with each of the newly independent states. And I decided to go to Ukraine first because of its symbolism. It is the place where the history of Russia began, and that's one of the reasons why Putin wants it back. Because he knows that is where the very idea of Russia began. Not the physical layout of Russia, but the concept of something called Russia — that began in Ukraine, in Kyiv. It was a hundred years before Moscow even began, as a village. Moscow did not exist. I knew this from the bits and pieces of Russian history which I know.

Our thinking about this long mission of mine began in 1991, just when the Soviet Union was dissolved and ceased to exist. And then we began to realize that there were new States that we had not really treated as independent States. And gradually the idea emerged in Washington that we should somehow ceremonially do something to recognize that we would have direct diplomatic relations with each of these states because they were going to be independent States. We would have to establish embassies in each of the new capital cities, and that would take some time.

That is when I was named as a special envoy, a mission which I started to carry out in 1991. It took me a whole year to carry it out, because what had been the USSR was so big, and included so many new countries. The idea was that I would travel to each of these new capitals with a special delegation, and in a ceremonial way I would open direct bilateral relations with each of these new states. So that's what I did. I assembled a small delegation and I had the use of an Air Force plane. I had a military entourage including a senior officer, so that I would always have a senior US military Officer in uniform right behind me.

I coordinated with the Embassy in Moscow. They were a bit hostile to my mission, because they saw it as losing bits of their own domain. The Embassy in Moscow had been covering all of these areas and they were now going to become separate, independent embassies, so the Embassy in Moscow was losing a huge amount of its empire as well. So some of the US diplomats in Moscow were not happy with my mission, which was designed to celebrate these independent states. They had an empire of their own to match the empire which the Russians had of all of these places, and so they were a bit unhappy to see another American Ambassador arrive on the scene. As far as they were concerned the Ambassador in Moscow was also the Ambassador to all of these places, and from time to time he went out to visit some of these places as the Ambassador. So, the Ambassador there was a bit hostile to my mission, and the whole Embassy was not really "going out of its way" to be helpful to me. I mean they weren't going to block my mission, obviously, because it had been ordered by Washington, but they also weren't going to make it really easy or important. They didn't want it to be important. So, I was up against that.

Anyway, I assembled a delegation, and actually one member of my delegation has now become a famous person. That was Marie Yovanovitch, the distinguished US Ambassador who was harassed by Trump when she was the Ambassador to Ukraine. My mission to the newly independent states took place while she was on her first assignment, which was at the US Embassy in Moscow. She was assigned as my special assistant from the Embassy in Moscow. She was still a junior officer at that time, but she speaks absolutely perfect, native Russian, and she was indispensable on this trip. I made arrangements in advance, and went one by one to all of these capital cities of the countries which had made up the USSR, and which had suddenly become independent.

My mission on this assignment was to pay a formal call on the Chief of State, or the local equivalent (sometimes the titles are different in these countries), the Prime Minister, and the Ministers of Defense and of Foreign Affairs in each of these new capitals. In each place the setup was a bit different, but more or less they all had people in these positions, so that was my mission. I used Moscow as my base, and also to send reporting telegrams to Washington, because we couldn't send any classified messages otherwise. And I had a small staff, including a military attaché. Military attaches are very important in such a situation because they're very visible. They wear their uniforms, and that's a visible indication that you're a senior American official. Otherwise, nobody knows who you are. And I carried out that highly-symbolic mission over the period of one year, because it was slow and somewhat complicated to line up each of these visits. The governments were new and were not used to visits by American Ambassadors, and often they did not know how to receive me, what to say, and what the "real meaning" of such a visit might be. And the first capital I went to was Kiev, because of the history – Kiev is the ancient birthplace of the very notion of Russia, the original "Kievan Rus" from which all Russian history flows. And Kiev is a big, well-developed, very sophisticated city, which gets a lot of visitors. And Kiev was not at all like the remote capital cities of Central Asia. Lots of people who visited Moscow would also go to Kiev, so the people there were pretty blasé (jaded) about foreign visitors. So, in comes an American (me) who says he is celebrating this and that. But it was just another American for them, so I think my reception there was not really very excited. I mean they were very polite, but they weren't excited, whereas in some places I visited the local people who were really very excited about seeing me, when they realized who I was and the symbolism of my visit. Many of these people had never seen an American Ambassador before, and surely some had never seen any sort of American! So, that was an interesting experience for me, both in terms of the countries concerned and the multiple experiences of all kinds. Later, after I retired, I went back to one of these places – Baku – the capital city of Azerbaijan, and lived there as a visiting professor at a local university for two years. Baku is really a wonderful place – beautiful, spotless, lively, historic, and open to the world, with great cuisine and excellent local wines!

You recently published a book "the Unknown Peace Agreement", formally known as the Joint Declaration of Twenty Two States, signed by their heads of state or government, including George H W Bush and Mikhail Gorbachev on November 19, 1990 in Paris. There you argue that it is the closest document we will ever have to a true "peace treaty" concluding World War II in Europe. How do these two documents complement each other and why do we all refer to the Paris Charter as the "peace agreement" of WWII?

Well, actually the "Joint Declaration of Twenty-two States" and the "Charter of Paris for a New Europe" are not really connected. They were simply signed in Paris at about the same time. The Joint Declaration is the Peace Agreement formally closing World

War Two in Europe, as I have explained in my book called "The Unknown Peace Agreement." And the reason it is a peace agreement is very concrete. We simply could not have such an agreement before then, and we couldn't have it after that moment in history. We could only have a legitimate peace agreement closing World War Two in Europe during a period of about six months, because not all of the States which were participants in that war existed before that period, and not all of them existed after that period. And for a legitimate agreement to end a war you need the same States to sign that peace agreement as the states that actually fought the war. This is the basic rule, the ancient rule for formally ending a war. As Hugo Grotius said: "Those who conduct a war are also those who must agree to end it, for each is master of his own interests and only he can dispose of them". In other words, unless the countries which actually fought the war are the same as the countries which sign the peace agreement, that agreement is just not valid. It's not a matter of choice. So, you have to have the countries that actually fought the war meet, and agree that the war is over, and to sign a document which says this. Other countries cannot agree to that—it must be the actual combatant countries. And so, in this case it had to be the countries which fought World War Two in Europe, and those countries only existed at the same time for a very short period. Germany was divided after the war, and until it was reunified it was not the same country that fought the war. The two Germanies were not the same as the single, united country of Germany. It had to be Germany that signed a peace agreement, and Germany was only reunified about one month before the signature of the Joint Declaration.

But that was not the end of the story. On the other side you had the Soviet Union, which was also one of the countries which fought the war. And once the Soviet Union broke up, you didn't have a legitimate country on the other side which could sign a genuine peace agreement, because you didn't have a state that was the same state that fought the war.

So the period during which you could conceivably have a genuine, legitimate, peace agreement for the war in Europe was very short. I can't remember now just how long it was, but it was six to eight months—something like that—or maybe as much as a year. But it was only during that period that it was possible to have a legitimate agreement to end that war. That's why it was so important, and that is why I was so scandalized to discover that it had not been noted anywhere. You could not find this explanation anywhere! That is why I wrote that book—because the true history on such a matter must be known.

I realized that this key point had been overlooked when a guy that I knew, who had interviewed me a number of times about all of this history—he was a professor at a university here in the States—published a book about the CSCE, or about Europe around this period, and he sent me a copy. I read through it, and I wrote him that "It's a very interesting book, but you have missed the fact that the Second World War was actually formally closed." He wrote back asking what I meant and I had to explain—The Joint Declaration—that is the function of the Joint Declaration. He had not heard of The Joint Declaration and had not even mentioned it in his book. Then I started doing bits and pieces of research, and I realized that nobody had recognized it!

So that's why I wrote this book—because I felt that it had to be known, it had to be announced. Even now nobody knows it and it's still overlooked. But the "Joint Declaration" is the one and only Peace Agreement which formally concluded the Second World War in Europe!

Already in the course of 1990, the spirit of cooperation and the joint aspiration of an inclusive and undivided European security were seriously threatened. For some the Charter was the end of the Cold War, for others it was not. Have these diverging narratives been sufficiently addressed or the lack of efforts to depoliticize history led to armed escalation in Ukraine? How much have competitive narratives, like Trump's "America first" contributed to Russia and China wanting to be "first", too?

What was lost through Trump's shifting of focus to Putin, is America as an ideal. Ronald Reagan talked about the 'shining city on the hill'. That was America, and we lost that. Largely because

of Trump, and people like Trump and issues that are Trump issues. The United States, even though it had bad practices, and had
minorities that didn't agree, still held out as an ideal "the best
kind of society". This was the 'shining city on the hill'. America
was that shining city on the hill, but with Trump all of the worst
traits in American society have come to the surface, and now you
can no longer claim that kind of image for the United States.
Where is it if not in the United States?

So, the world has lost something that it had, which was this
image of the shining city on the hill. We've lost it. And that's because the United States has lost it. Partly because of Trump. It's
still out there in many ways that are not Trump, but unfortunately
Trump epitomizes all the negatives in our society in a way that
pulls them all together, which creates an image that you can see,
and you can see where it's going, where it's going to go. You can
see its effect and that it has a huge following. It has become concrete, scary, in ways that it wasn't before. With Trump the negative side of our society has become much worse than it was before,
and that is a tragedy for our country, for America.

**What kind of diplomacy will we need in the period after the war
in Ukraine?**

The alternatives to the United States are unfortunately few and far
between, because there is no other country in the world which
brings together the stature, the size, the variety of national origins,
and the worldwide influence that the United States has. There
isn't anything else like the United States. There are some similarities — Canada, for example, has many traits, but it's not a big power. There are certain places, countries that have certain things that
are relevant and similar. But there's nothing that brings it all together as an image like the United States, and unfortunately, that
image now has been completely decimated by Trump, and could
be even worse if Trump were to have some sort of comeback; and
even if he doesn't have a comeback. It will linger for a long time,
because he made it into a national kind of thing and even made it
respectable for a lot of people who came out of hiding, and now

are public about these things. And so right now we have no 'shining city on the hill'!

We need to rebuild, following the Trump era, which still hovers over us. We need, once again, to find that "shining city" — or some other image which meets the needs, the dreams, of the world. What other country can do that? We will have to find a leader who thinks in those terms, who can bring the country together again, so that it can, once again, inspire people everywhere.

What is more difficult is to look beyond the specific issues and problems of today, and to find — in all the disappointing history which we know — some redeeming quality, some ray of hope for the future, which can restore our faith in our own (the human) race. That is very difficult when one has seen the cruelty of dictatorial regimes, "up close and personal". We have not yet found the basis, nor the means, to rid our governing systems of bullies, thieves, and tyrants, and I do not think we will find those answers any time soon.

Maybe the hope then should not be in leading countries or leading politicians, but in investments we have to make now — investment in the future through the students that we have in our classrooms, or in efforts to mobilize young people to be politically more active and to care about what is happening in their political systems? Maybe we will not see another superpower being a leader and maybe small-scale initiatives, like 'Fridays for Future' will guide social justice and responsible governance. Can youth and civil society help overcome the divisive narratives in times when consensus has become impossible even on holding a Human Dimension Implementation Meeting (HDIM)? What can they do?

That is a possibility. What you are saying is that it is possible for things to evolve gradually, and I think that is generally true.

So, yes, things may evolve positively in the USA. That has always been the hope and I think that continues and could grow. But right now we are still in a very bad period because it is not certain that Trump is out forever. There is a very real possibility that he could regain the Presidency, and that puts the US in a very ambiguous, very dangerous, middle ground, where we don't know how our country may evolve.

It would be nice to be able to say: "Look, this is the United States; we will always come back to our basic values." But I don't think it is possible to say that now with full confidence. Our experience in recent years has not been very reassuring. Certainly, there is a lot of wisdom in being patient, in the belief that solutions often come in smaller units, and if we can succeed, for example, in establishing systems that are fair and forward-looking, even in just one country, that's a huge victory. Maybe it's better to start that way—and to try to change things patiently and gradually. But it will take a lot of determination, and patience.

OSCE has had a very limited outreach programme and usually only in the countries where there are field operations. What can we teach the young and politically curious minds and how?

The OSCE has done very little to explain to the public how, and why, it came to exist, what became its objectives, and the benefits which it brought to international relations in Europe, including North America. This failure has had the effect of negating many of the benefits, and potential benefits of such an organization. Certainly, the primary objectives, and benefits of such an organization must be better mutual understanding among the people of the countries which are its members, and certainly such mutual understanding is badly needed in Europe, including the adjacent areas of the Mediterranean and Central Asia. And one can argue that we have now come full circle, and are back at the very East-West hostilities which the CSCE-OSCE was intended to ease and even overcome. Our stated objectives in those negotiations were to develop friendlier, more open relations between East and West in Europe, in many domains, and while that appeared to be working at the time, it quickly was lost, and now East-West relations, at least with Russia, are once again at rock-bottom. And the CSCE-OSCE is nowhere to be seen.

There are, of course, many reasons for this situation, and for the way East-West relations have deteriorated in recent years, and the fault for this deterioration certainly does not lie in the CSCE process, its institutions, or its objectives. They lie in the failure of at least one state—Russia—to accept those objectives, and to pursue instead more self-serving, nationalist aims. In spite of the availability of the CSCE as a bridging organization involving all the European countries, one country—Russia—has deliberately followed a self-serving path, and has set out to re-establish its own area of domination, even the complete re-absorption of its near neighbors, in what is clearly an effort to re-create the whole of the Soviet Union, with Russia in control of that entire area. It can be no surprise to anyone that the—quite substantial—nation of Ukraine has refused to accept such Russian domination, nor that most of the rest of the World has supported Ukraine in this resistance.

So the agreements and understandings which formed the basis of the "Helsinki" process have been dramatically set aside by Putin's Moscow, which has broken all those agreements and is now pursuing a ruthless war of aggression against its neighbor, Ukraine. Faced with this situation virtually the whole of the rest of Europe, and many other neighboring states, are strongly supporting Ukraine, and we are all looking forward to the demise of the current Russian leader. When he disappears, perhaps Europe can resume its efforts to maintain a peaceful international order throughout its region, and can try to continue in the direction of peaceful, mutual respect among the nations of Europe, including Russia. That is the only positive, worthwhile, course for Europe to follow.

Just a word about the Prague office of the OSCE. This was my personal idea—one of quite a number which I contributed over the years! I got to know the small library which was there, which I used for quick research on a number of issues, and thought it would be useful for the OSCE to have a center where diplomats could do the research which is always essential in international relations. At the time we were looking for ways in which the CSCE could be useful to the member states, and I thought a place for concrete research on issues would be useful in that sense. So many issues arose during our negotiations which required some research that such a facility was clearly needed—especially for foreign diplomats who may be here on assignment and suddenly need to understand the background of some international issue. The idea was popular among the CSCE delegations, and it was immediately adopted. I hope it has fulfilled its mission over the years!

I have always believed that diplomacy requires a full understanding of the issues—not just a superficial knowledge of events, but much more than that—an understanding of the sensitivities, the complexities, the implications and the risks of international activities of all kinds. And that sort of understanding demands a deeper feeling for the way things work, of the effects of actions taken, of the way such actions may affect the lives of ordinary people.

Are we facing a new polarization and how can research and diplomacy help find a better way out of it, so we can have a new Paris sooner rather than wait for 45 years (which is the period between the end of the WWII to Paris)? What would you recommend for better healing and building anti-fragility systems for the shocks not to rock our core in the future?

In a way we reached a high point—at least in the diplomatic dimension—with the Summit in Paris and the "Charter of Paris" which was signed there. Those negotiations, and the summit-level commitments they produced, gave us an agreed context, within the framework of the CSCE: agreed principles which must be respected, the basic requirement for respect for human rights, and agreement on the need to avoid conflicts which, after all, was not nothing! And all of Europe was committed by these agreements. The CSCE was thus a central, a pivotal element for the World, which included the commitments of all of Europe and its off-shoots, including the United States and Canada, and we were discussing the very basic values we believe in. We were negotiating, discussing how to express them as something we could all agree on, and would commit to. That's what the principles are all about—respect for the universal values and principles which all of our nations share. And if one looks back on that, in comparison with where we are now, it's just phenomenal. The text of the Helsinki Final Act starts with these universally-recognized principles, and these principles are very much a statement of the values which we in the West believe in, subscribed to by all the countries of Europe and North America. And it is simply incredible that we all agreed to them, committed our countries to respecting them, including the USSR and all the nations of Europe, both East and West!

We are at a really low point in our relations with Moscow right now, and it is hard to see how we can climb back to some level of mutual understanding. There isn't really a lot of evidence out there that will point toward moving in a more positive direction...certainly not in my lifetime. I certainly won't see anything like the "Helsinki" agreements again. The contrast with the period of those agreements is very dramatic, very striking. Imagine what we were able to agree on with the Russians at that time, and where we are now....

The organization symbolizes what is the very best in Europe, and which is somehow totally ignored. Europe is the essence of a broad variety of nationalities, of nations which have many things in common, and also many things which are individual and national, and belong very much to their nations. The continent is filled with such things — music, literature, traditional clothing, ancient sayings, and endless traditional stories. It is what makes Europe so interesting, so fascinating. This complicated region with its multiple languages and cultures and national identities has been attractive with these fascinating central features, the reason why everyone, from all parts of the world, wanted to come to Europe, to see it, hear it, experience it. And this has also been its weakness, because it meant rivalry and, at times, war.

As this is an oral history project, and has the element of intergenerational dialogue, I would like to share an important lesson for the young scholars and activists, and that is: wars are destructive and cruel, and no one benefits from them; they must find ways for Europe to avoid wars. That was our principal objective in creating the OSCE, and we must pursue it in every possible way. That, as I said in one of my books, is the lesson of Helsinki. There are many things which young people can learn from the history of Europe, and hopefully those lessons can help us to avoid more wars in — and over — Europe.

I was born in Europe, at a time when the continent was headed toward war. My father was Italian, but my mother was American. When she was convinced that war was inevitable, she risked her life to take her two children to America. Our ship arrived in New York just as the war was beginning, as Hitler invaded Poland. I grew up as an American, and I never saw my father again — he passed away before my family could be reunited. My story is one of many, many stories which tell us that wars must be avoided, that we must do everything possible to avoid them. I spent my career as an American diplomat, negotiating for this objective, and I would gladly do it all over again.

You have a personal connection with all the topics that you were trying to put behind in the CSCE negotiations. You suffered from the war in which you lost a lot. Many years later you became the lead negotiator in the negotiations which formally concluded the war. Tell us how important were these negotiations to you personally? How did the two-year old Italian boy who had to escape Europe on the last ship from Genoa to New York become the chief US negotiator working for decades on closing that same war?

My family and I are among those who were devastated by World War Two in Europe, which was what we were trying to put behind us in the Helsinki negotiations. In the Helsinki negotiations we were trying to close that war — find normal relations among the countries concerned. And I was not just an "outside expert" brought in to carry out these negotiations — I was one of those who had suffered from the war — I lost my family, my home, my nationality, my identity, because of that war. And the supreme irony was that, many years later, I became the central person, representing one of the main powers, the USA, in the negotiations which formally concluded that war, and which ultimately made it possible for Europe to return to a normal situation. That little Italian kid became the chief US negotiator in closing that war!

I was born in Stresa, in the north of Italy, in a villa surrounded by the gardens of an historic luxury resort — The Grand Hotel Des Iles Borromees. The Hotel is an iconic landmark on the shores of Lago Maggiore and it figures in Ernest Hemingway's novel "Farewell to Arms". My father, Franco Maresca, was a long-time Director of the hotel and as all male Italians were subject to possible national service as war loomed in Europe, he was not permitted to leave Italy. He took us to Genoa where we took the ship to New York and that was the last time we saw my father. As the Conte di Savoia was pulling away from the pier, out into the Hudson River, empty and without passengers, to return to Italy and the war, my mother, with her two small children, passed through the US customs and immigration services, where the official looked closely at my mother's American passport, in which the US Consul in Milano had inscribed her two small children (age 2 and 4), with our photos. We were entered into her American passport, which meant that we were also Americans, as prescribed by the American Consul General in Milano. All the other passengers had left, and the ship was slowly backing away from the pier, which was empty. And we were still standing in front of the US immigration officer. My mother was very nervous and concerned, so she said to the immigration official, very softly, "Please, can you tell me, what is the nationality of my two children?" He did not reply immediately, as he looked through her American passport, where he saw our two photos, stamped with the official seal of the US Consulate in Milano. After a pause, the immigration official said: "Lady," — and he stamped her passport — "As of now, they're American citizens."

My mother, with her two infants, and dragging our luggage, walked to the nearest hotel. It was evening by then, and they had a vacant room. My mother and sister slept in the bed, and I, as the smallest, slept in two chairs, pulled together, with my mother's mink coat as my blanket. We were in America, and we were Americans, but we had nothing but the "clothes on our backs". It was the beginning of a whole new life—of struggle and poverty, and never seeing my father again.

Maresca's father, Franco Maresca, in the gardens of the Grand Hotel des Iles Borromees, of which he was the Director, walking his dog in the winter snow.

STRESA BORROMEO - GRAND HOTEL ET DES ILES BORROMÉES

Sailboats on the lake, Lago Maggiore, in front of the Grand Hotel des Iles Borromees, where Maresca was born and lived until 1939, when he left with his mother for the USA, as Italy went to war.

My story is the classic story of America — its promise to everyone who has ever arrived here. They have all arrived with nothing, typically not even speaking English. We did this quite literally, even though my mother was American (she had been living in Italy for ten years). Years later that little Italian boy, fleeing the war and speaking not a single word of English, became the American Ambassador who negotiated the formal conclusion of that very war!

Furthermore, for me, the CSCE negotiating process was an extraordinary opportunity to do what diplomats are supposed to do, but which in practice they almost never actually get to do, which is to negotiate about war and peace. Of course, negotiations to bring peace, or to stave off war, are the absolute peak of the broad range of activities which diplomats get into in their careers, and very few diplomats ever actually get to negotiate on true issues of war and peace. And even if they are eventually included in such negotiations, their real roles are usually limited to specific, very narrow, subjects. But my role in the CSCE process was very different, because from the beginning I was acknowledged as the experienced expert within the delegation, and took the leading role, both in our relations with Washington and, more importantly, in contacts with key delegations, most importantly, of course, the delegation of the USSR.

My first assignment was the usual rotating assignment which every in-coming junior diplomat in the US system goes through — six months in each specialized type of work at an overseas post. So I was, first, the Vice Consul at the US Consulate in Amsterdam, then, second, a commercial officer in the economic section of the US Embassy in The Hague, then an economic officer and finally a political officer. And then I was transferred back to Washington to be the junior French Desk Officer (tracking US relations with France). My French was just short of perfect, which impressed everyone, so one day I was urgently sent out to the airport to keep Charles De Gaulle, then the President of France, company while he awaited his plane, which was late. I spent an hour with him — just the two of us plus the French Ambassador in Washington, and this gave me a VERY big reputation!

But at a certain point, shortly after my meeting with De Gaulle, I was called in my office in Washington and asked if I was available for an interview with the Secretary General of NATO. "When?" I asked. "In about 30 minutes," was the reply. So, I was interviewed by the Secretary General of NATO, an Italian, called Manlio Brosio. The interview lasted about ten minutes, and I was the only candidate the US presented for the job as his "Directeur de Cabinet." (I spoke fluent French and Italian—both of which were requirements for the job). He approved my assignment immediately and I left one week later for NATO HQ in Brussels. That is where I learned my life-long trade specialty, which was negotiating with the Soviets. At NATO I was immediately plunged into the Alliance's secret preparations for some sort of negotiating process with the USSR. NATO decided to send Brosio to Moscow as its "Explorer" to explore with the Soviets whether there might be a serious basis for some sort of negotiating process to lower the level of military confrontation in Europe. Brosio chose me as the single person who would accompany him on that trip to Moscow, which really launched me on the East-West negotiating track. But the trip to Moscow never happened. The Soviets included a brief sentence in a hugely long communique from Moscow which said that the USSR "would not negotiate with a representative of a military alliance." Brosio was super-smart, and he spotted this sentence immediately. "That is their response," he said, and began packing his bags to return to Torino, his home city. He knew that phrase meant the Soviets would not deal with him as "the negotiator," for ending the Cold War. So, our mission ended before it began, after more than a year of preparations at NATO!

Having in mind the reaction to the signing of the HFA, what was in your opinion the perception of the signing of the Charter of Paris in the USA? How did the politicians react and what was the public reaction to it?

When the Helsinki Final Act was signed, the reactions in the USA were mainly negative. The Wall Street Journal, for example, famously headlined, on their first page, "Jerry Don't Go!" (Addressed to President Gerald Ford, who traveled to Helsinki to sign the Helsinki Final Act.) But years later, when Europe had evolved into the "detente era," and East-West relations had significantly improved, the same newspaper actually apologized for that headline, explaining that they now recognized that relations with Russia (under Gorbachev) had improved.

Personally, I was skeptical about the whole set of "Helsinki" negotiations. But I also believed that it was better to negotiate and to try to find elements of common ground than to just face off and maintain negative relations. The US Administration had failed to explain the meaning of the Helsinki Final Act, and what we were trying to achieve by lowering the level of confrontation with Moscow. And later, when the "Helsinki" negotiations actually accelerated the reunification of Germany and the opening of more positive East-West relations, I think the Helsinki negotiations earned their recognition as a positive factor. The Charter of Paris was generally seen positively, partly because Gorbachev personally was seen that way. I was proud to have led that negotiation.

Unfortunately, Putin has now ruined all those efforts to find common ground, and to build something more positive and beneficial for everyone. Surely there will be possibilities in the future to rebuild peace between East and West in Europe, but it will require the removal of Putin — at a minimum — and considerable effort to rebuild some level of mutual trust.

What was your role and what was the composition of the US delegation that carried the Charter of Paris negotiations? How did that happen? Was there a strategic outreach to particular experts, were people sent from the capital or diplomats who were nearby were assigned?

When I returned to Washington from my assignment as the "Minister" (Deputy to the Ambassador) at the American Embassy in Paris I was named as an Assistant Secretary of Defense, in the Pentagon. I was the Assistant Secretary Responsible for Europe. It was a senior position which was not at all a part of the regular assignment pattern for State Department Foreign Service Officers like

myself, and it irritated a lot of people that after my unusual assignment to Paris I was recruited for this—also very unusual—
assignment to a senior position in the Pentagon. So, I knew that
"the system"—the State Department personnel system—would be
out to "get me" when I was up for another assignment. From their
perspective I had been named to those assignments "outside of
the system."

When the time came for me to move on to another assignment, I did a little research to find a negotiating position in my area of expertise, with Ambassadorial rank, and "expressed my interest" in being assigned as the Ambassador and negotiator for
military confidence-building measures. This was a small negotiating position for which I had ideal experience—in Europe and negotiating essentially with the Russians. The negotiations were to
open in Vienna soon, so after I had been confirmed by Congress I
went to Vienna and set up my office and residence there.

There were two negotiations going on in parallel in Vienna at
that time. The one which was considered the more important one
in Washington was the negotiation on Mutual and Balanced Force
Reductions (MBFR) in Europe, which was seeking concrete agreed
force reductions on the basis of "balance" between the two sides.
This was very difficult because it meant essentially that the Eastern side would have to make bigger reductions than the Western
side. The US Delegation for those negotiations was headed by a
political appointee, Jim Woolsey. The MBFR negotiations included
only the Delegations from the member countries of NATO and the
Warsaw Pact. The other negotiation in Vienna was the one in
which I was the Head of the US Delegation. This was about military Confidence and Security-Building Measures (CSBMs), a subject which had been included in the Helsinki Final Act and was
the established military component of the CSCE agenda, having
produced more than one agreement since Helsinki. This negotiation included delegations from all the states which were participants in the CSCE, even the neutrals and the mini-states.

Then, Gorbachev and Mitterrand had their summit meeting
in Crimea, and agreed that the full CSCE should be re-convened,
to move toward greater East-West cooperation. The French moved

very quickly, and before anyone could develop opposition to the concept, the negotiations where I was the US Ambassador were up-graded to be the preparatory negotiations for the newly-arranged, forthcoming, summit-level CSCE Meeting, to be negotiated in Vienna for a summit-level signing ceremony in Paris.

I was, of course, already the US Ambassador to that very negotiation, and so I just expanded my responsibilities, as well as the number of people in my delegation. And later, negotiation of another important historical landmark came under my responsibility — from some perspectives even more important than the others. This was the negotiation of the formal agreement that World War Two in Europe was over, and that all the countries of Europe and North America were no longer enemies. All the countries which had been involved in World War Two in Europe signed a new agreement — called the "Joint Declaration of Twenty-two States" — at the summit level, in Paris. So, the negotiation of that agreement was also under my responsibility. I think almost all of the Ambassadors who were in Paris for the start of this broad range of negotiations simply expanded their responsibilities and continued their work, perhaps adding one or two experts to their delegations to cover all the subjects. But it certainly became a complicated, swiftly-moving set of issues, covering all the major questions relating to Europe at the time, in agreements which were to be signed by the Chiefs of State of Europe and North America. It might have been daunting — but we did not have time to think about it, so we just moved forward to carry out those negotiations.

What were the core aspired goals of your Delegation and what were the concessions you had to make in order to get to the end line? Was the Charter what you wanted or more could have been achieved?

The goals shifted in major ways when Mitterrand and Gorbachev agreed to co-sponsor a new Summit-level meeting of the CSCE in Paris to sign the documents which we were negotiating in Vienna. That decision meant that we had to produce a broad — and significant — document which would be appropriate for signature by the

Heads of State of Europe and North America — it would have to clearly merit a summit-level signature. And it was clear that the only subject which could clearly fit that role, at that moment of history, would be the official closing of the Cold War. So, we negotiators immediately turned our focus to developing that sort of document.

In fact, we really needed two new documents. In Vienna there was already a negotiation going on which was aimed at producing an agreement on the reduction of NATO and Warsaw Pact forces in Europe. And in the CSCE context we were already negotiating a broad document intended to encourage a general opening of friendly east-west relations in Europe, which eventually was given the ambitious title of the "Charter of Paris for a New Europe." But we realized immediately that we would need another document for that summit to make sense; we needed a document which would formally close World War Two in Europe.

At that time the situation in Europe had been rapidly evolving, and with Gorbachev as the leader of the USSR, it was possible to think in these terms, and to negotiate positively with the Soviet representatives. In addition, all the legal elements for officially closing World War Two in Europe were satisfied in our gathering in Vienna. Everyone recognized that, for the first time, we could actually think in terms of an official "war-closing document" which would officially conclude World War Two in Europe. So, we immediately faced the challenge of producing a true war-concluding document for World War Two in Europe. This started in private, even secretive, meetings of "Ambassadors only," in obscure conference rooms in the Hofburg Palace in Vienna, and produced a new document which was given the deliberately modest title of the "Joint Declaration of Twenty-two States". I have written a book about the negotiation of this document — called "The Unknown Peace Agreement." Strangely, this document has remained in the background, so I decided to write a book, to explain its meaning and how it originated, which was published in 2022.

But even with that book now published, the way World War Two was officially concluded remains relatively obscure, which is unfortunate, and I think it is high time for scholars and so-called experts to recognize this key historical document with the overly-modest title of the "Joint Declaration of Twenty-two States." Historians have a responsibility to confirm this key element of recent European history!

And that document is also an important part of the answer to your question: the "Joint Declaration, although it was NOT anticipated before we started the negotiations to prepare for the summit in Paris, became one of the principal achievements of those negotiations: it was the official conclusion of World War Two in Europe! And it is the only such document, for a very simple reason: the USSR — one of the principal participants in that war, was dissolved shortly after the Vienna negotiations, so any agreed, official conclusion to the war, which would have to include the USSR as a major participant in the war, became impossible after the USSR was dissolved. That leaves the "Joint Declaration" as the closest thing we will ever see to a true "peace agreement" closing World War Two in Europe.

I have said this before, specifically in my book, "The Unknown Peace Agreement," but I repeat it here: The "Joint Declaration of Twenty-two States" is the sole, and genuine, "peace agreement" which officially concluded World War Two in Europe, and, as far as we can tell, there will never be another such document, in view of the fact that one of the key participants in that war — the USSR — was dissolved and ceased to exist shortly after the "Joint Declaration" was signed.

The Charter of Paris was of course important in its own right — it made possible a broad opening of East-West relations in Europe, the effects of which were truly historic. That coming-together in Paris marked the official — and also the practical — end of an era: the era of the Cold War. And as a part of that change of historical eras, it also made possible the official closing of World War Two in Europe, thru the signature of the Joint Declaration. That summit-level meeting in Paris deserves to be recognized as the symbolic turning point which it was, in the history of Europe, and the world. I have always thought the Paris summit meeting has been "undervalued," historically. It was a true — and positive — historical turning point. Perhaps we can see that more clearly now, with Gorbachev long-gone and with Putin having trashed many of the agreements and standards we had begun to take for granted. And now Putin has started down a dangerous new path, and we cannot really see where this new path will lead us.

What did you expect to be the main change in the way CSCE was working after the Charter of Paris was adopted?

I don't think I had any clear idea of how things would develop in the immediate aftermath of the Paris summit. We had all worked very hard and quickly to complete what was then called the "Charter of Paris." Unlike most of my colleagues in the CSCE, I had a long experience of working within the NATO secretariat, as the "Chef de Cabinet" of two Secretaries General of NATO, one Italian and one Dutch, which gave me some very relevant experience. So, I foresaw an on-going CSCE assembly and an international staff — something similar to the NATO set-up, which includes a large, permanent, international staff, and national delegations which are available to participate in regular meetings among the representatives of the member states.

Of course, in the NATO context the member states are all formal allies, through the NATO treaty, whereas the OSCE includes both allies (members of NATO and also the European Union) and also at least potential enemies: Russia and its close allies. So, the areas of cooperation — or even full openness — were always bound to be much more limited than in the NATO context. But I knew from my experience at NATO that cooperation within an on-going institution can bring some surprises, and, especially when Gorbachev was still the Soviet leader, it was possible to imagine some positive developments.

But we also have had experience of working together in multilateral organizations which include hostile states, even declared enemies — for example within the UN context. I think international relations can also be carried out, at times, with joint, positive objectives, even when direct relations are not very positive. Sometimes you have to work in such situations, in this world, and make the best of it! And sometimes such situations can yield surprisingly positive results, even if they are modest.

The results of such international negotiations may sometimes seem modest, but they can bring small changes, and those changes are important. Positive changes must be pursued consistently, with determination and patience, and they take time.

Of course now, with Putin's aggression against Ukraine, we are in another era, and it will take a lot of changes to get back to the comparatively positive situation we had when Gorbachev was the Russian leader. We will have to pursue that effort with a lot of determination and patience.

What lessons would you share with the current diplomats dealing with Ukraine? Have you been invited to advise the current decision-makers in Washington, Vienna and elsewhere?

Ukraine is the victim of a deliberate, savage, bloody and unscrupulous aggression by Vladimir Putin. It is a classic "aggression for conquest," and breaks all the relevant rules and agreements. And it is part of Putin's broad, on-going effort to regain Russia's control over the whole of what was the USSR — the job he was handed when Boris Yeltsin introduced him, at the time of the dissolution of the USSR, as the person who was mandated to re-assemble that empire.

This is a very long story, and we are just in the middle of it. The rest of the world must oppose Putin and his plans — because they are directly contrary to any notion of international law or civilized, peaceful behavior among sovereign, independent nation-states. Putin's Russia has become a broad threat to peaceful coexistence among the countries of East and West, which needs to be stopped.

I have not been invited to advise anyone, but these are my independent views, based on my experience in the region, and my long years of facing, negotiating, and working with the Soviet Union and Russia.

What is the way forward for the OSCE?

The OSCE took form during a period when relations between the West and Moscow seemed to be improving—it would not have been considered a rational venture without the broadly-believed idea that our relations with the Soviet Union were improving. And the CSCE—its format and its agenda—now appear to be far removed from the current relationship with Russia. The CSCE relationship depended heavily on an assumption that Russia was acting in good faith, that it would respect its commitments, and that it had as much interest in improving relations, and in a full and stable peace, as we did.

I think that has now been shown to be untrue, which means we must return to the sort of suspicion and mistrust which dominated our relations with Moscow in the past. That is clearly the case as long as Putin remains in power, and will probably continue when Putin is replaced by a successor—unless and until Russia proves convincingly that it can be trusted to respect its commitments. And I would argue that—even then—we should maintain our ability to defend ourselves.

People will debate for a very long time over whether this return to confrontation was predictable or not, whether it was naive to seek more positive relations with Moscow, or we should have continued to maintain the distance and mistrust of the Cold War period. I was a leading negotiator during the "detente" era, following my years as a military officer and a key official in the NATO structure, and then I participated in our efforts to improve relations and to seek rational commitments, to find and maintain a stable peace between East and West in Europe. I don't think we were naive in that effort, and I am still in favor of seeking every possible opening to build a rational and lasting peace, while maintaining our ability to defend our interests if and when that may be necessary.

It is never easy, politically, to carry out both of these objectives at the same time, but I think we must do exactly that. The objective of finding a rational and solid basis for peace is simply too important to just brush it aside because we are disappointed, or because we do not trust the other side. On the contrary — we must pursue peace in spite of, and fully recognizing, those difficulties, taking them into account and protecting ourselves in case our efforts for peace should fail. We need to find the basis for a stable peace precisely because we are faced with an on-going threat of possible war. That is the reason for our efforts, which must continue.

The interview with Amb. John J. Maresca was conducted by Ida Manton in 2022/23 as part of an extra-budgetary project "Living Memory – 30th Anniversary of the Charter of Paris for the New Europe". This is a project of the OSCE's Documentation Center in Prague (DCiP).

John Maresca and Ida Manton

Annexes

I.   Joint Declaration of Twenty-two States

II. "The CSCE at its Inception; 1975 in Myth and Reality" – OSCE Yearbook, Hamburg, 2005

III. "Russia's 'Near Abroad' – a Dilemma for the West" by John Maresca. First Published in: "Crisis Management in the CIS: Whither Russia?" Hans-Georg Ehrhart, Anna Kreikemeyer and Andrei V. Zagorski, eds. © Nomos Verlagsgesellschaft, Baden-Baden, 1995. Reprinted with kind permission.

IV. "The End of the Cold War is Also Over", Summary of John J. Maresca's Lecture Series at Stanford University, Published by the Center for International Security and Arms Control, Stanford University, 1995

Annex I

JOINT DECLARATION OF TWENTYTWO STATES
PARIS, 19 NOVEMBER 1990

The Heads of State or Government of Belgium, Bulgaria, Canada, the Czech and Slovak Federal Republic, Denmark, France, Germany, Greece, Hungary, Iceland, Italy, Luxembourg, the Netherlands, Norway, Poland, Portugal, Romania, Spain, Turkey, the Union of Soviet Socialist Republics, the United Kingdom and the United States of America

- greatly welcoming the historic changes in Europe,
- gratified by the growing implementation throughout Europe of a common commitment to pluralist democracy, the rule of law and human rights, which are essential to lasting security on the continent,
- affirming the end of the era of division and confrontation which has lasted for more than four decades, the improvement in relation among their countries and the contribution this makes to the security of all,
- confident that the signature of the Treaty on Conventional Armed Forces in Europe represents a major contribution to the common objective of increased security and stability in Europe, and

convinced that these developments must form part of a continuing process of cooperation in building the structures of a more united continent,

Issue the following Declaration:

1. The signatories solemnly declare that, in the new era of European relations which is beginning, they are no longer adversaries, will build new partnerships and extend to each other the hand of friendship.

2. They recall their obligations under the Charter of the United Nations and reaffirm all of their commitments under the Helsinki Final Act. They stress that all of the ten Helsinki Principles are of primary significance and that, accordingly, they will be equally and unreservedly applied, each of them being interpreted taking into account the others. In that context, they affirm their obligations and commitment to refrain from the threat or use of force against the territorial integrity or the political independence of any State, from seeking to change existing borders by threat or use of force, and from acting in any other manner inconsistent with the principles and purposes of those documents. None of their weapons will ever be used except in self-defense or otherwise in accordance with the Charter of the United Nations.

3. They recognize that security is indivisible and that the security of each of their countries is inextricably linked to the security of all the States participating in the Conference on Security and Cooperation in Europe.

4. They undertake to maintain only such military capabilities as are necessary to prevent war and provide for effective defense. They will bear in mind the relationship between military capabilities and doctrines.

5. They reaffirm that every State has the right to be or not to be a party to a treaty of alliance.

6. They note with approval the intensification of political and military contacts among them to promote mutual understanding and confidence. They welcome in this context the positive responses made to recent proposals for new regular diplomatic liaison.

7. They declare their determination to contribute actively to conventional, nuclear and chemical arms control and disarmament agreements which enhance security and stability for all. In particular, they call for the early entry into force of the Treaty on Conventional Armed Forces in Europe and commit themselves to continue the process of strengthening peace in Europe through conventional arms control within the framework of the CSCE. They welcome

the prospect of new negotiations between the United States and the Soviet Union on the reduction of their shortrange nuclear forces.

8. They welcome the contribution that confidence and securitybuilding measures have made to lessening tensions and fully support the further development of such measures. They reaffirm the importance of the "Open Skies" initiative and their determination to bring the negotiations to a successful conclusion as soon as possible.

9. They pledge to work together with the other CSCE participating States to strengthen the CSCE process so that it can make an even greater contribution to security and stability in Europe. They recognize in particular the need to enhance political consultations among CSCE participants and to develop other CSCE mechanisms. They are convinced that the Treaty on Conventional Armed Forces in Europe and agreement on a substantial new set of CSBM's, together with new patterns of cooperation in the framework of the CSCE, will lead to increased security and thus to enduring peace and stability in Europe.

10. They believe that the preceding points reflect the deep longing of their peoples for close cooperation and mutual understanding and declare that they will work steadily for the further development of their relations in accordance with the present Declaration as well as with the principles set forth in the Helsinki Final Act.

Annex II

John J. Maresca:
The CSCE at Its Inception: 1975 in Myth and Reality[1]

I confess to having had a thirty-year love-hate relationship with the CSCE.

Perhaps I am unique among those who were responsible for the negotiation of the Final Act of 1975 because of my long association with the CSCE in the years that followed. After the Final Act was signed in Helsinki, I returned to Washington to head the State Department office responsible for the CSCE. In that capacity, I pursued the commitments of the Final Act by establishing an annual report on their implementation and pressing NATO to commission a similar report. I then returned to the first follow-up meeting of the CSCE in Belgrade in 1979. I published a book entitled "To Helsinki"[2] on the negotiation of the Final Act. And I returned once again to the CSCE as head of the US Delegation when the Conference re-convened in Vienna in 1989. In Vienna, we negotiated the "Charter of Paris for a New Europe", signed at the Summit in 1990 to symbolically close the Cold War.

On the one hand, my involvement in the CSCE was clearly one of the dominant experiences of my diplomatic career. But the ambiguity of American views towards this sprawling negotiating process, the political battles related to it in Washington, and the effects of all this on me personally, left scars each time I worked directly with the CSCE. And the ups and downs of successes and dead-end failures in the CSCE process itself have been difficult not only to judge, but also to live through.

It was always professionally and psychologically danger-ous — a kind of high-wire act — because the American negotiators

---

[1]   First published in: OSCE Yearbook 2005. Institute for Peace Research and Security Policy at the University of Hamburg (IFSH), p. 29-38. © Nomos Verlagsgesellschaft, Baden-Baden. Reprinted with kind permission.

[2]   John J. Maresca, *To Helsinki: The Conference on Security and Cooperation in Europe, 1973-1975*, Durham, NC 1985.

had virtually no instructions, no real communication with the political leadership in Washington and no back-up. If you made a
misstep, there would be no one there to catch you. And in the end
it became physically dangerous too, at least for me.

In the early 1990s I flew "nap of the earth" style into war
zones in the Caucasus in rickety old Russian Army helicopters.
"I'll be back at five o'clock", my Russian Army pilot said to me
once, as I disembarked on a CSCE mission in the middle of God-
only-knew-where. "And I'll wait for five minutes." Few people in
Washington knew what I was doing, and even fewer cared. The
result for me has been that, while sharing the fascination that other Helsinki hands have felt for this sporadic negotiating process, I
have also tried to distance myself from it.

***

It was August 1975 in Helsinki and I was indeed "the only American who understood what was going on in the negotiations", as
the Assistant Secretary of State for European Affairs, Arthur
Hartman, put it to Henry Kissinger at the time of the Summit. And
Hartman was right—I understood it all: the complex relationships
between the different issues, the key personalities involved, what
was at stake and how to resolve the various Gordian knots so that
the result would be acceptable. The Final Act was acceptable, it
was done and Gerry Ford and Leonid Brezhnev and all the others
signed it.

Unfortunately for me, the CSCE was always something of a
political football in Washington—the Republicans embarrassedly
disowning it despite the fact that the main events happened on
their watches; the Democrats trying hard to blame the Republicans for ignoring the CSCE's potential, while also trying desperately to take the credit for making it work, particularly with respect to Russian Jewish emigration and East European hopes for
independence, issues that resonated among the American electorate.

Looking back over the thirty years that have passed since the
Final Act was signed, during many of which I was deeply involved in CSCE negotiations and activities, I ask myself again that

question we all posed in Helsinki in the summer of 1975: What is the real significance of the Final Act?

This remains the central question for those of us who participated in the negotiations, who observed them and measured the results against the historical forces at work in Europe at the time. The heart of the matter is the extent to which this negotiation, this event, this document, this historical episode, had something to do with the unraveling of the Communist system in the USSR and its satellite governments in what was then called Eastern Europe.

The specifics of what was negotiated were modest, especially to the experienced analytical reader. In the autumn of 1975, I was invited to speak on the Helsinki Final Act to an assembly of interested professors at the Harvard Faculty Club. The first question after my presentation was from an indignant professor who had only heard of our negotiations when President Ford announced that he would participate in the signing: "Why were we not informed that these negotiations were going on?" In reply, I said that everything we were doing was public and that at least two American professors I knew had followed the negotiations closely, out of personal interest. The real question, I threw back, was why American academics in general, so focused on nuclear negotiations and other strategic matters, were not interested in our conference.

A second, only slightly more respectful question was this: "With all this paper, all this complex language, was this two-year negotiation really worth it?" As it happened, just the week before the State Department had arranged for the reunification of two Czechoslovak children with their parents, on the basis of the family reunification provisions of the Final Act. I told the story, and then added: "If one child is reunited with his or her parents because of our effort, then it was worth it."

But such reunifications were rare, sporadic successes in a much broader situation, which had not changed, and did not change in any fundamental way for another dozen years.

It is tempting, now that the Cold War is over and Europe has evolved into such a different place, to exaggerate the importance of the Final Act and its role in bringing about the historical changes that took place towards the end of the century. I have heard many people do this, especially those who were involved in the CSCE negotiations of that period. It is also tempting to exaggerate the importance of the roles played by oneself or one's group. I have also observed this recently, at so-called "oral history" sessions, and in myself, too. But is it correct?

Certainly the CSCE had its place in the historical evolution of that time, but was it a force for change or a reflection of it?

The content of the Final Act is, in fact, rather thin. Taking a look at what was vaunted by the Western group at the time as the Basket Three "Family Package" of freer travel, marriages between nationals of different states, family contacts, and reunification, one wonders why these modest points should have been considered so threatening by the Communist countries that they resisted accepting them at the negotiating table for two years. And the Final Act's simple allusion to human rights must be contrasted with the fact that human rights were already laid out very fully in the Universal Declaration of Human rights of 1948, which is legally binding for all signatories of the United Nations Charter, unlike the commitments of the CSCE, which were purely political. The CSCE really added very little to the existing obligations in this field.

And yet the Soviet Union did indeed ferociously resist every positive adjective, every clarifying comma, and carefully sought to add qualifiers and weaken the verb forms to avoid any sense of real obligation in the "freer movement" sections of the document. The Soviets, so it appeared, deeply feared those adjectives and verb forms. The reality was that the low priority attached to these initiatives by Western governments, particularly the administration in Washington, had led the Soviets to conclude that they did not need to accept them and could get to Helsinki without doing so. These "freer movement" ideas had been dreamed up and drafted on paper at the working level, primarily in the Political Committee at NATO, in Brussels. While they had been officially endorsed by Western governments, no senior Western political personality was in a position to argue them out with the Soviet leadership.

The Soviet Basket Three negotiator took advantage of this situation. He was a master of the techniques of bullying, ridiculing, and humiliating his Western counterparts and did so whenever possible. He held the line against all those threatening stronger adjectives and verb forms right up to the last moment. He even resisted the urging of his fellow delegation members, even the chief of his own delegation. This was recounted to us regularly by his colleagues in the corridors of the negotiation and afterwards. And it was also noted in an article I published in 1996, in the now-defunct magazine "Transition", by the chief Soviet negotiator, Anatoly Kovalev, shortly before his death. The Soviet Basket Three negotiator resisted those adjectives until he was overruled by the Kremlin and the Politburo of the Communist Party itself, at the very last moment, in order to make way for the Summit Meeting in Helsinki that Leonid Brezhnev so ardently wanted. Why such fierce resistance? It seems absurd today. Ironically, though, it almost did not matter what we put into the Final Act. All of our efforts on specific proposals and airtight wording were irrelevant. What mattered — perhaps the only thing that mattered — was that there *was* a Final Act and that it seemed to represent some sort of consensus agreement on human rights and "freer movement of people and ideas". As we learned in the months and years that followed, the dissidents in the USSR and Eastern Europe would have agitated on the basis of almost any CSCE document. And it was, finally, the agitation of the dissidents and the yearnings of ordinary people that brought down the Communist system.

This real impact of the Final Act was only revealed later, and it was both dramatic and singular, as well as complex, multifaceted, subtle, and unexpected. What we found as the Cold War drew to a close was that the Final Act had created a new dynamic, based on a newly universalized set of values. And, perhaps most importantly, it had created a new dimension, a new space, in which to pursue these values.

The Final Act created a new space, a space in which new kinds of events were possible. And we did not realize this until history demanded such a space, because the events that took place later were unthinkable in 1975.

***

The drama came in Central Europe in the sultry summer days of 1989. At that time, a number of East Germans, on vacation in Hungary, sought exit visas to cross the border into Austria. They knew that if they could reach the West German Embassy in Vienna, a short distance from the Austro-Hungarian frontier, they would immediately be issued West German passports, and be free. Free.

The Hungarian government, itself evolving in response to popular demands, was caught in a dilemma. A bilateral treaty with the German Democratic Republic (GDR) precluded it from issuing such exit visas to GDR citizens without the prior consent of the GDR government. But Budapest's reading of the Helsinki Final Act was that the Hungarian government was required to allow persons to leave the country if they wished to do so. For whatever combination of reason and rationale, the Hungarian government decided that it was more important in 1989 to respect their commitments under the Final Act than it was to respect their bilateral obligations to the GDR. The result was that thousands of East German vacationers joyously crossed the border into Austria and made their way, as fast as they could, to Vienna and the West German Embassy. At the time, I was the American ambassador to the CSCE meeting in Vienna, and I well recall the astonishment and pleasure we all felt at seeing those tiny East German "Trabant" cars left by the side of the road. The East German families that had been driving them simply abandoned them when they ran out of gas, and hitchhiked the rest of the way to Vienna and the West German Embassy, where the queues of passport applicants stretched around the corner.

But those East Germans abandoned more than just their cars. They were so anxious to reach freedom that they left behind all of their possessions, their apartments, and their relatives, without any real hope of ever seeing them again. It was a moving historical moment. One could sense that this was indeed the tiny trickle coming through the dyke and that the dyke itself would collapse very soon.

Events rushed ahead that year as East Germans clambered over the walls of the West German Embassy in Prague, leading to the collapse of East Germany, of Soviet domination of Eastern (now again called Central) Europe, and even the disintegration of the USSR itself. My Austrian colleague sent me a section of the demolished barbed wire fence that had sealed the frontier with Hungary. I still have it, twisted and rusty, in my office. Farmers once again began ploughing long-unused fields that crossed the border.

In 1989, I participated in a meeting of American ambassadors in Europe, held in Berlin, where the discussion was on the implications of these events. Most of the ambassadors present thought that Moscow would crack down and suppress this latest round of agitation for freedom, as it had in the past. But three of us, Henry Grunwald, Dick Walters, and I, argued that there was something different at work here and that it would be very difficult for the Soviets to walk this cat back.

Even more surprising developments began to take place in this new space. One day, Albania, isolated from the rest of Europe since the 1940s, asked to become a member of the CSCE. In Vienna the Conference was caught by surprise by this unexpected démarche. Albania had been invited to join the original CSCE negotiations in 1973, but had never responded; no one doubted that they were eligible to join. But how to admit them to the CSCE space after so much had happened on the basis of commitments taken years before?

The key ambassadors conferred at the Hofburg Palace, where the CSCE met. We decided we needed a "snapshot", meaning a report, of conditions in Albania at that moment, to be able to judge how the country would implement its commitments after becoming a member. But how to do this on behalf of the CSCE? Easy, I told my German colleague, since Germany held the rotating CSCE Chairmanship at the time: We will send a CSCE mission to Albania to report on conditions there. How can we do that, he responded; the CSCE has never had a mission. If we decide to do it,

I said, we can do it. That was the first CSCE mission. Since that time CSCE missions (now sometimes called "centres" of "offices") have multiplied all over Europe and Central Asia, with different mandates and wide-ranging specialist staffing, giving the CSCE an entirely new dimension for encouraging respect for its values. I was sent to Albania and the Newly Independent States as a special envoy, to evaluate the situation on behalf of the United States and to explain the basis for our bilateral relations. I met with the leaders of these governments, most of them quite surprised to find an American ambassador in their midst. In Tirana, the defence minister, a sophisticated engineer in his fifties, told me I was the first American he had ever seen.

The Charter of Paris for a New Europe, signed in 1990, established the CSCE's Office for Democratic Institutions and Human Rights (ODIHR) in Warsaw, an important institution in its own right, which now helps to ensure, through election monitoring and other devices, that the democratic and human rights standards optimistically referred to in the Final Act of 1975, and in later CSCE agreements, are respected in practice.

Another example of what was made possible by the creation of this new dimension through the Helsinki Final Act was an obscure but important document called the "Joint Declaration of Twenty-Two States". This document, negotiated in the lead-up to the Paris Summit of 1990, was signed at the Elysee Palace by all the members of NATO and the Warsaw Pact. It declared that the Cold War was over, and that there was no longer any reason for hostility among them. If there is a document that confirms that the Cold War was over, this "Joint Declaration" is it. Such a document could perhaps only have been negotiated in the unique CSCE space.

The Final Act had also held the door open for the reunification of Germany, through its language on possible peaceful changes of borders: "They [the participating States] consider that their frontiers can be changed, in accordance with international law, by peaceful means and by agreement." This sentence was negotiated personally by Andrei Gromyko and Henry Kissinger on behalf of the West German government, for this specific purpose.

As one striking example of the low esteem in which Washington held the CSCE, the negotiation of this key clause of the Final Act was ridiculed publicly by Kissinger as a negotiation over the "placement of commas", though it was the placement of the two commas in this phrase that gave it its full significance: changes in frontiers *are* in accordance with international law if they are brought about by peaceful means and mutual agreement.

When the Cold War ended, there were indeed many changes in European frontiers, some peaceful, some convulsive, as history caught up with the evolutions that had taken place between 1945 and 1990. In Germany, in the USSR, in Yugoslavia, and in Czechoslovakia, borders were changed. Some established states disappeared, some new ones appeared, and some old ones reappeared. Of course, the Final Act was not used as the basis or the rationale for the actions that led to these national changes, but the Final Act nonetheless did foreclose many questions, or even possible obstacles, that might have been raised against them. One day, my East German colleague, whose place at the conference table, in alphabetical order, was right next to mine, told me he was saying goodbye. He was an engaging man, to whom I had once tried to explain what "market forces" are. We wished each other well, as ambassadors do when one is transferred. But the next day there was no longer an East German at our conference table.

And the CSCE had not yet reached the limits of how it could surprise and respond to new developments. When the USSR dissolved into independent republics, the first issue posed for the CSCE was how to treat the Newly Independent States that had been parts of the USSR. The answer was clear for those new states that were physically within geographic Europe—Lithuania, Latvia, Estonia, Belarus, Ukraine, and Moldova, plus of course Russia. They were indisputably eligible for CSCE membership. But what attitude should the CSCE adopt towards the new states of the Caucasus and Central Asia—Georgia, Armenia, Azerbaijan, Kazakhstan, Turkmenistan, Uzbekistan, Tajikistan, and Kyrgyzstan?

Many Europeans argued that these new countries were "not European" and therefore could not rightly belong to a European conference. But my view was that these countries had been members of the CSCE from the beginning as parts of the USSR, which was one of the Conference's original participating States. They had thus already accepted and were bound by the commitments of the Final Act, unless they chose to renounce them as independent countries. So not receiving them as CSCE participating States would be tantamount to throwing them out, an action for which there was no justification.

Moreover, I argued that if these countries had the vocation to adhere to the Final Act's commitments, we should welcome that and seek to ensure that these commitments were respected after independence. In the end, these new countries were all invited to join the CSCE in their own right, and today the OSCE and its missions (or centres or offices) are active throughout these states, and in former Yugoslavia, giving the new states important ties with Europe and the West.

It can be argued, I believe, that the evolution of these states since their independence has been influenced by their membership of what is now the OSCE. OSCE observers from ODIHR in Warsaw have watched over and commented on their elections (as they have also done in the most recent American presidential election), and OSCE Centres and Offices in many of these states offer a glimpse of the system of values recognized in the Final Act. That these Newly Independent States should be linked—even by so fragile a thread as the OSCE—with transnational standards of human rights and democratic governance is a positive element for their development. Indeed, we have heard echoes of Helsinki in events in the Baltic states, in the Caucasus, and most recently in Ukraine, as these countries have pursued their destinies. Even the much ridiculed "arms control junk food" of CSCE military security commitments, the so-called Confidence and Security-Building Measures (first called Confidence Building Measures, CBMs, which later evolved into CSBMs), have had a certain underappreciated importance. This family of modest gestures towards military *détente* first appeared in the Final Act and was developed and expanded in later CSCE negotiations. It was in one of those later negotiations that agreement was first reached on a no-notice military inspection regime between NATO and the USSR, opening the door to other such inspection regimes in relation to nuclear missiles and conventional forces.

The CSCE has had its failures, too, but that is to be expected. The Final Act contained hopeful language on the peaceful settlement of disputes, later developed into a "mechanism" for resolving interstate disagreements. But this has remained on paper only, and the CSCE mechanism has never been used for specific dispute resolution.

It is true that the CSCE has sometimes been able to enter situations in a "good offices" role, when other organizations could not. This was true, for example, of its missions to Chechnya. But it has not done well at conflict mediation thus far. I can bear witness personally to this, since I was a part of the CSCE's first mediation effort—between Armenians and Azerbaijanis in relation to the conflict over Nagorno-Karabakh. That initiative, oddly called the "Minsk Group", is still going on, still without any real success. This mediation, which was politically—and also physically—dangerous at a time when the vicious conflict in the area was still raging, has been a failure, at least thus far. Or is this failure actually because the United States government has not really pressed for a settlement, in view of its own conflicting political interests in the region?

When Yugoslavia began its descent into the inferno of ethnic cleansing and ruthless civil conflict, the CSCE was unable to muster an adequate response. There were discussions in CSCE meetings, and resolutions were passed. But in those early days, the United States thought this should be a "European problem", and pushed the European Union to take the lead in dealing with it. And the Europeans, who could not even agree on a general approach, were slow, inept, and lacking in the essential political will. Under the circumstances, the CSCE was reduced to adding some symbolic CSCE representatives to the EU's all-but-useless "observer force".

But perhaps the CSCE and its varied emanations have avoided conflicts, which have not surfaced because of the efforts of its institutions. This was the intent of the CSCE in establishing a position called the High Commissioner on National Minorities. The two persons who have held this position, former Dutch Foreign Minister Max van der Stoel and, currently, Rolf Ekéus, a Swedish diplomat, have concentrated their work in countries where there is potential for internal conflict, and their interventions have apparently had positive effects. While it is of course impossible to know what might have happened without these efforts, even if only one conflict has been avoided this would be no small achievement in view of the number of wars that have broken out in Europe after the close of the Cold War.

***

How should we understand this vast panorama of events in the CSCE's "space", which opened in August of 1975 and has not yet closed, though shifting priorities may yet sideline it? In my book about the negotiation of the Final Act, I suggested that the Final Act was a kind of ersatz peace treaty, substituting for the formal peace treaty, which would most likely never be signed, to close the Second World War. Now, many years later, I realize that I was at least partly wrong. My analysis at that time was too simple, too instantaneous, and perforce did not take account of the evolution that has taken place in the thirty years that followed.

The way I would summarize it now is this: The Final Act opened a vast political and historical dimension of opportunity, in which it became possible to settle the remaining issues from World War II. The Cold War, it now appears, was a lingering and long-unresolved final battle of that war. Only when the Cold War battle ended was it possible to say that the Second World War had truly been closed.

The "peace treaty" ending the Second World War is, in fact, a complex of documents that includes the Final Act, the Charter of Paris, the Joint Declaration of Twenty-Two States, the agreements on German reunification, and many other less central instruments. And now, when one can move freely across the German plains through Poland into Ukraine and even Russia, Europe is indeed whole again, free of the legacies of the war.

Much of this history took place within the new "space" created by the Final Act. Perhaps it would be an exaggeration to say it could *only* have taken place after the Final Act. The peoples of Europe are really the force that changed the situation from that of the Cold War to what Europe has now become. But I believe it is fair to say that the progression was eased thanks to the effects of the CSCE.

***

From the time in 1973 when George Vest called me to ask if I would join him in the US Delegation to the negotiations in Helsinki, I was fascinated by the CSCE. I have always had a great admiration for Vest, a truly talented and original multilateral negotiator, with a folksy style all his own. "If you just sit there, and are prepared to listen to people," Vest used to say, "people will come and talk to you." I can see him now, straddling a backless leather bench in the lobby of the CSCE Conference Centre, with other ambassadors circling about, waiting to have a word with him. And perhaps, after all, this is the main strength — and the legacy — of the CSCE: a place where people will listen, and therefore a place where people can talk. Is this a modest achievement, or is it the key to finding solutions?

Annex III

Russia's "Near Abroad"—A Dilemma for the West[1]

1. The Breakup of an Empire

Years ago, I met a French civil servant in a small port city on the West coast of Africa. He told me he had been in a town in the interior when the country had gained its independence, as he passed the railroad station, he noticed a festive crowd patiently waiting in the hot midday sun, and asked the station master why so many people were there. The answer was this: "They know Freedom is coming today, and they know it is important, so they assume it will arrive by train."

When the rotting structure of an empire ultimately begins to crumble, the process of breakup is always pretty much the same. Neither the colonial populations nor the people of the mother country are prepared, politically or psychologically, for the separation, and the result is a protracted period of struggle. There is violence in the colonial areas and a mass exodus back to the mother country. Economic chaos is pervasive, and bitterness in the mother country leads to nationalistic rear-guard actions aimed at preventing or reversing the colonies' progress toward independence. In the colonized areas the struggle is often fratricidal as a new national identity is forged; political alliances are formed or broken, and minority groups within a colony sometimes try to capitalize on the moment to seize their own freedom.

In most cases, this period of struggle has preceded the independence of the colonies, although some aspects have tended to continue into the post-independence period as well. The Russian/Soviet empire was not immune to these symptoms. But instead of experiencing this period of struggle primarily before the independence of the colonies, in the Russian case it is happening

---

[1]   First published in: "Crisis Management in the CIS: Whither Russia?" Hans-Georg Ehrhart, Anna Kreikemeyer and Andrei V. Zagorski, eds. © Nomos Verlagsgesellschaft, Baden-Baden, 1995. Reprinted with kind permission.

largely after their nominal independence. In fact, Russia and its former empire—the area which Russians like to call their "near abroad,"—is going through this period of struggle now, and will probably take years, possibly decades, to complete the transition. All of the features of exodus, bitterness, economic chaos, rearguard actions and fratricidal competition have already appeared in some areas, and will surely emerge elsewhere before the process has run its course.

In Moscow political leaders are wrestling with the problems posed by this period of struggle. Ironically, the situation parallels in many ways the circumstances which followed the Bolshevik revolution, when many of the areas which had been colonized by the Czars also broke away from Russia and enjoyed brief periods of independence. The Bolsheviks used a variety of techniques then to regain control over the breakaway republics, just as Moscow is doing now in a classic effort to resist further movement toward real independence for the former Russian colonies.

2. The Russian Concept of Peacekeeping
There is little agreement in Moscow as to how this should be done, or even whether it is a good idea. Although millions of Russians believe it was a mistake to let the "near abroad" go, there are also many Russians who are aware that recovering Russia's dominance of these former colonies will mean that Russia will once again have responsibility for them too, at a time when each one of them is frought with complex problems and the Russian government is having enough trouble just keeping Russia itself united and economically viable. But as often happens in periods of difficulty, aggressive nationalism appears to be winning the debate over the proper role for Russia in the so-called near abroad. As a consequence, there has been no objection to the fact that the defense ministry has taken the lead, ostensibly with the purpose of restoring order and ensuring security on Russia's frontiers.

The Russian defense establishment, badly demoralized by its humiliating withdrawal from Eastern Europe at the end of the Cold War, has been an armed force without a mission since the collapse of communism, which formed its ideological justification and gave it a purpose. Now it is being positioned, politically and psychologically, to be the defender of the ethnic Russian populations in the newly-independent states and the imposer of stability everywhere on the territory of the former Soviet Union. This has given the Russian army a palpable new sense of purpose.

The world's image of the Russian armed forces is of an underfunded, illhoused and unprepared military organization which is no longer a threat to international security. This may be the case on the strategic level, with an important caveat for Russia's nuclear arsenal. But within the former USSR the Russian army still looms larger than life. Russia's armed forces have 2 million men under arms, the full range of equipment, and a tough approach to problem-solving which is often reflected in the comments of their leader, defense minister Pavel Grachev.[2] This is a military force which is capable of intervening anywhere in the former USSR, and has already done so with relative success in Tajikistan, Georgia and Moldova.

The Russian army has interlinked bases, command, control and communications channels, and supply routes throughout ex-Soviet territory. It controls mountains of weapons and ammunition supplies, plus "volunteers" and cheap mercenaries of every technical specialty. Its officer corps is a far-flung fraternity (which always had very few members from the distrusted Asian and moslem ethnic groups) that still has enormous influence in every defense ministry among the newly-independent states. Furthermore, the old KGB intelligence networks are still largely intact, and very little can happen in the vast ex-Soviet space without it being known in the defense and internal security ministries in Moscow.

The military and its backers like to think of all their operations in the so-called "near abroad" as peacekeeping, and apparently believe that they should be backed and even paid for by the

---

[2]   See, for example, Grachev's statement before a negotiating session on Nagorno-Karabakh that "Whatever I propose, that's what we're going to agree on," cited in Elizabeth Fuller, The Karabakh Mediation Process: Grachev versus the CSCE?, RFE/RL Research Report, Vol. 3, No. 23, June 10, 1994.

international community at large. But the Russians have developed their own concept of peacekeeping which is quite different from the classic definition, and which contrasts sharply, not only with the longstanding practices of the United Nations in this field, but also with normal relations among independent states.

The Russian concept of peacekeeping is really more like forceful suppression of violence than it is like the impartial and pacific approach of international organizations. Even the expression, when used in Russian, means something different.[3] Concretely, Russian troops engaged in such operations are authorized to use force not only to defend themselves if they are attacked, but also to suppress violations of the peace, whatever the cause. UN peacekeeping missions are only authorized to use force in self-defense. Russian peacekeeping also does not put the same stress on the negotiation of stable political solutions as is the case in international operations. Suppression of violence is itself a goal. For the international community peacekeeping is only an unavoidable expedient which may help to make it possible to organize a rational political negotiation to find a resolution to the underlying dispute. In this approach the goal is clearly the achievement of a negotiated political solution, not just the suppression of violence.

The Russian approach grows naturally out of the historical experience of the Russian and Soviet armed forces with respect to security problems within the USSR. When such problems arose, the army was sent to impose order. They often accomplished this objective brutally, and in some cases the legacy they left behind only complicated and embittered the underlying dispute. Many historians contend that in fact the deliberate policy of Stalin was to keep local hostilities alive, or even to create or fuel them, in order to ensure that distant parts of the Soviet Union would always be dependent on the Center for their security.[4] A part of the dilemma for the West is the possibility that Russian peacekeeping troops

---

3   See, for example, Therese Raphael, Russia: The New Imperialism, The Wall Street Journal, June 22, 1994.

4   For a detailed analysis of the Russian approach to peacekeeping, in contrast to that of the West, see Pavel K. Baev, Peacekeeping as a Challenge to European Borders, Security Dialogue, Volume 24(2), pp. 137-150.

would use intimidation or force to suppress elements they considered unfavorable to Moscow's interests, just as Soviet forces did before them.

Coupled with the Russian interpretation of their peacekeeping role is a strongly-held view that maintaining peace and stability on the territory of the former USSR is the exclusive prerogative of Russia. This view, too, resembles the possessive attitudes of virtually all colonial powers with respect to their former colonies, but is perhaps felt even more strongly in the case of Russia because of the country's historic xenophobia, particularly toward the West. Many Russians see their country as having a unique role across Eurasia, and do not believe outsiders have any place in this area.

Current Russian suspicions of outside attempts to settle problems in the former USSR have come out most strongly in the behavior of Russian representatives with regard to the conflict over the mountain enclave of Nagorno-Karabakh, in the Trans-Caucasus. This is because this is the one conflict on former Soviet territory in which an international body—the "Minsk Group"—has been mandated to find a solution. Here the Russians, led by defense minister Grachev, have made a concerted effort to undercut international initiatives, to keep the international community out, and to resolve the problem themselves, using their own troops, as a way of ensuring their domination of the region. The Russians have appeared prepared to accept accusations of bad faith in this instance, as the price of ensuring exclusive Russian predominance.[5]

The development of the Commonwealth of Independent States (CIS) has helped to provide a facade of international cooperation in dealing with conflicts within the former USSR. In cases where there has been international interest, such as Georgia, Azerbaijan and Tajikistan, the Russians have made a point of calling their proposed peacekeeping interventions CIS operations, even when participation by non-Russian CIS members was no

---

[5] For background on the Nagorno-Karabakh dispute see "War in the Caucasus: A Proposal for Settlement of the Nagorno-Karabakh Conflict," Special Report, United States Institute of Peace. 1994.

more than symbolic. Russia has tried to establish the CIS as a recognized international organization equivalent to, say, the European Union. Their effort has been to obtain international acceptance that the CIS has exclusive competence for dealing with conflicts on the territory of the former USSR. All CIS operations would, of course, be dominated or possibly even exclusively manned, by Russia.

Russia's tendency toward keeping the international community out of the former USSR appears to date from late 1992 or the beginning of 1993, and was perhaps signaled to the world by foreign minister Andrei Kozyrev's "mock speech" at the Ministerial session of the CSCE in Stockholm in December of 1992. Kozyrev gave such an aggressive, hard-line speech that his listeners were shocked. It closely resembled Soviet speeches of the sixties or seventies. With respect to the "near abroad," Kozyrev said that "The space of the former Soviet Union cannot be viewed as a zone where the CSCE norms can be applied in full. This is in effect a post-imperial space where Russia has to defend its interests by all available means, including military and economic ones. We shall firmly insist that the former republics of the USSR immediately join the new federation or confederation, and this will be discussed in no uncertain terms."[6] An hour later, possibly because journalists were sending off dramatic reports of the event, Kozyrev took the floor again to explain that it was all a hoax; he just wanted to show his colleagues what Russia's policies might be like if hard-line nationalists gained power.

Yet the policies of the Yeltsin government began to evolve rapidly from that time, especially on a few leading edge issues such as the role of the international community in resolving the Nagorno-Karabakh war. Before 1993 was over Kozyrev's "real" policies closely resembled the hard-line nationalist policies of his "mock" Stockholm speech. In particular, Russia's determination to

---

[6]   Moscow News, December 16, 1992.

regain control over the whole of the former USSR had become obvious to all but the most naive Western observers.[7]

The world became conscious of the evolution of Russia toward an aggressive nationalism only when Vladimir Zhirinovski made a strong showing in the Russian parliamentary elections in the autumn of 1993. Some analysis have suggested that the Yeltsin government adjusted its policies because of the electoral strength Zhirinovski showed at that time. But in fact the evolution of policy began much earlier, and what the appearance of Zhirinovski really revealed was the growing depth and breadth of nationalist feeling in Russia as it progressed through a period of economic and political retrenchment.

The general state of disarray in Moscow makes it difficult to find any really credible, authoritative and complete statement of Russian policy toward the newly-independent states of the former USSR. It may be that there simply is no centrally-developed or approved policy concept or list of policy objectives. Rather there may be an accumulation of separate actions by different ministries, all seeking to reflect and anticipate what they see as the tendency of political opinion. And all receiving at least the tacit approval of president Yeltsin.

But by observing Russian actions and the aims which Russian negotiators have pursued in their dealings with the new states, it is possible to draw up a representative list of policy directions. Based on this crude revival of Kremlinology, the Russians appear to want to:

- Control the outer frontiers of the whole of the former USSR. The Russians point out that there were no marked or even surveyed internal borders in the former USSR, and to establish them now would be very costly.[8] By their logic, a better solution is simply to re-establish the old frontiers, and man them with Russian border forces. Cur-

7 For another view of Russia's expanding efforts to regain control of the see Bruce D. Porter and Carol Saivetz, The Once and Future Empire: Russa and the 'Near Abroad,' The Washington Quarterly, Summer, 1994

8 Raphael, op cit.

rent exceptions to this general rule include the Baltic States and Azerbaijan, but in the latter case the Russians are actively pressing for re-introduction of their border guards along the frontier with Iran.

- Maintain military bases throughout the former USSR. After the Russians forced Eduard Shevardnadze to capitulate and invite Russian forces into Georgia, the only areas where Russian basing is in question are, once again, the Baltic States, where Estonia and Latvia are still struggling to get the Russians out, and Azerbaijan, where the government clearly does not want the Russians to come back. Russia is currently exerting strong pressure on the government of Azerbaijan to agree to the reopening of their large base in Gandzha. The other new states never managed to get rid of the Russians.

- Exercise economic and financial control. This is being accomplished in most places through the CIS economic and financial agreements, under which each newly-independent state yields to Russia key decision-making powers. But this process could also be dangerous for the Russian economy, since loading the failing economies of the new states onto the economic disaster of Russia itself could bring even greater problems.

- Control natural resources throughout the former USSR, particularly energy resources. Not only does Russia itself need these resources, it also knows that they are a prime source of hard currency, and could emancipate some former colonies from Russian control. The Russian technique for gaining control over resources is not very subtle; Russia simply demands a share, and is also insisting that pipeline routes from the Caucasus and Central Asia should cross Russia.

- Keep the international community out. For Russia the international community means the United States and its surrogates, and Russian xenophobes are determined to exclude American influence, as well as Turkish or islamic influences, to which Russia is particularly sensitive along its southern frontier.

- Finally, the Russians are determined to preclude a breakup of the Russian Federation itself, the 'empire within an empire,' which includes many colonized peoples. Some peoples within the Russian Federation have already demanded, and received, greater degrees of autonomy for their regions, drawing inspiration from the actions of minority peoples in the "near abroad." The favored technique for ensuring control over Russia is to re-establish control over the whole of the former USSR through consolidation of the Russian-dominated CIS. This would re-establish the traditional buffer zones and theoretically insulate the Russian Federation from such potential instabilities.

As part of their effort to obtain recognition of their special role in the former USSR, the Russians have attempted to equate their activities there with US activities in the countries of America's 'backyard,' such as Haiti, and French activities in countries of special interest to France, such as Rwanda. Russia's linkage of these issues in negotiations within the UN Security Council resulted in American agreement to an ambiguous UN acceptance of a Russian/CIS peacekeeping force for Georgia, in return for a Russian non-veto on the Security Council resolution approving a US-led invasion of Haiti.[9]

It should be noted that the Russians have few qualms about interpreting any international community statement relating to their "peacekeeping" roles as something of a mandate. Their troops in Tajikistan have worn the familiar sky-blue colors of the UN, even though they have never been given a UN mandate to do so. Thus, even an ambiguously-worded UN decision on the force in Georgia will be used by the Russians as a full UN endorsement.

---

[9]   There has been little reporting in the press on this incident. One of the few articles to appear at the time was Lally Weymouth, Yalta II. The Washington Post. July 24, 1994.

3. The Western Dilemma

Russia's deliberate juxtaposition of the Russian role in Georgia against the US role in Haiti and the French role in Rwanda has posed more starkly than ever before the dilemma of the appropriate Western attitude toward Russia's activities in the so-called near abroad. This attitude has been equivocal up to now.

The reasons for this Western ambiguity seem to be, first, that the West is not prepared to undertake peacekeeping in much of the former USSR. Westerners therefore do not consider themselves in a position to criticize the only country—Russia—which is ready to step in, regardless of the Russians' methods or motivation. Second, many in the West have been hopeful that an emerging democratic Russia would not revert to an imperialist policy. These people have believed that giving Yeltsin the benefit of the doubt in the 'near abroad' would encourage him to show a greater sense of responsibility. The facade of the CIS, as thin as it may be, has also confused many westerners who may not have perceived the very real differences between this emerging mechanism for a new Russian domination and the European Union's democratic structures.

In addition, Western countries have become more reluctant to intervene in post-Communist disputes after their experience in ex-Yugoslavia. Their priorities currently include the maintenance of stability in nearby regions and the avoidance of conflicts which are likely to send further waves of refugees as immigrants toward their shores. For America this refugee-phobia is focussed on Asia, Latin America and the Caribbean. But for Europe it is concentrated on Africa, the Middle East and South Asia. Instability in the former USSR can only add to these problems. Islamic immigrants are viewed with a particularly wary eye in Europe, although this aspect is seldom highlighted.

At the same time, Russia's effort to obtain recognition as the mandated peacekeeper for the 'near abroad' tends to force the issue, especially when the Russians compare their role with Western peacekeeping practices, as in Haiti or Rwanda. The first question is whether or not Russia's justification for its interventions, and its actions in carrying them out, differ from those of Western countries in similar circumstances. If there are such differences, the question then becomes whether or not Russia's actions in the so-called "near abroad" are acceptable, and if they are not, what might be an appropriate Western response.

The issue is a broad one, posing moral, political and practical issues. Perhaps the key factor to bear in mind is that the whole of the former USSR, as noted above, is engaged in a colonial struggle associated with the breakup of the Russian/Soviet empire. With this aspect in mind, the differences between Russian peacekeeping in the 'near abroad' and Western-sponsored peacekeeping operations is clearer.

The Russian relationship with the new states of the former Soviet Union is still in the very sensitive phase of anti-colonial struggle and separation of a colonial mother country from a set of colonies. Russian interventions in this area cannot be distinguished from attempts to simply prevent or forestall independence. Such interventions touch all the sensitivities which dominate a period of decolonization, and are as likely to exacerbate problems as they are to resolve them. Even if violence is stopped through the threat of Russian force, this will only prolong the suppression of nationalist feelings which caused the problem in the first place. While the US relationship with Haiti, and the French relationship with Rwanda do have similarities with post - colonial relations, neither is in the immediate period of anti-colonial struggle.

Also, neither the US nor France seeks a permanent place in these countries; indeed, much of the debate in both Washington and Paris has concentrated on the problem of how to get out once an intervention has been undertaken. Issues relating to how to conclude an intervention and withdraw are among the key criteria for intervening at all in the US Administration's policy on peacekeeping interventions. In contrast, the Russians seek a permanent military presence.

Nor have the U.S. or France sought to integrate the countries in which they intervene into a state-like structure controlled by them, especially against the will of the country concerned. But that is precisely what Russia has been doing in pressing Georgia and Azerbaijan to accept Russian troops and join the CIS. This extraordinary behavior resembles forcible conquest more than it does the peacekeeping concepts of the end of the twentieth century.

Moscow has pressured Georgia (and Azerbaijan) for a variety of permanent concessions such as bases, border guards and agreement to Russian dominance of economic policies, while refusing to put its intervention forces under the discipline and control of an international organization, such as the UN or the CSCE, which would then be able to decide the eventual date of departure of the Russian contingents. These factors make it difficult to accept that the Russian peacekeeping operations are comparable in any way to international operations, and it was certainly a mistake to allow Russia to equate them, even tacitly, during the UN Security Council negotiations.

4. A 'New Yalta Line' for Europe

Nonetheless, the ambiguity of the Western attitude remains. Does the West, in fact, feel more comfortable with a new Yalta-style division of spheres of influence and responsibility, especially if it is only implicit and is not overtly stated? Perhaps. Of course no Western country could agree to a formally-recognized division. But, sadly, the evidence to date is that, provided the 'new Yalta line' is pushed Eastward from the line which divided Cold War Europe, an implicit division is being quietly accepted.

The reason is simple realpolitik: no Western country is prepared to undertake interventions of any kind in Central Asia or the Caucasus; they do not want to see conflicts in those areas go unended; and all would prefer to give Russia the benefit of the doubt (or turn a blind eye) and let the Russians handle the complex problems of these regions by themselves. Thus there is indeed an implicit 'new Yalta line' beyond which stabilizing responsibilities are seen as belonging to Russia.

Where then does the new dividing line fall, differentiating those areas which are sufficiently interesting to the West to warrant its intervention when needed, and those areas which are not that interesting? This is not yet entirely clear, and may take some time to be pinned down. There are three possibilities, under which:

- Central and Eastern Europe outside the territory of the former USSR are of interest to the West, but the countries on the territory of the former USSR are not;
- Central and Eastern Europe including the Baltic States are of interest to the West, but the other countries of the former USSR are not; or
- Central and Eastern Europe including the Baltic States, Ukraine and Moldova (and possibly Armenia and Azerbaijan) are of interest to the West, but the other countries of the former USSR are not.

It is not yet clear which one of the above descriptions will best define the emerging Western consensus about a 'new Yalta line' for Europe. While it may sound cynical to discuss the issue in these terms, that is unfortunately the practical implication of recent Western policies.

The key Western policy decision thus far has been NATO's adoption of the "Partnership for Peace" program. This program ostensibly equates all the countries of Europe and the former USSR in terms of their potential relationship with NATO. Austria or Poland theoretically has the same potential for developing a close relationship with, or joining, NATO as Kyrgyzstan or Tajikistan. This is clearly absurd, and the net effect of the Partnership for Peace program has therefore been to postpone the difficult decisions about which countries would be close to, or join, NATO, and fall on the Western side of the new line, and which countries would not develop such close relations, and would find themselves on the Eastern side of the line. Since Russia itself cannot join NATO without destroying it or at least rendering it meaningless, the Eastern side of the new line will obviously be a Russian-dominated area.

The Partnership for Peace thus reinforced the security vacuum in which the countries of Central and Eastern Europe have been left. The resulting sense of doubt and uncertainty, far from its stated purpose of creating a Europe without dividing lines, actually adds to the instability of the present equation and multiplies the temptations to Russian nationalists to reassert themselves in these areas too.

Of the states of the former USSR, the Baltic States have been clearest in stating that they want to become a part of the West. The likelihood is that, given their special history and Western outlook, they will continue to receive moderate Western support. Even the Russians, by agreeing to withdraw their forces from the area, appear to have accepted this as inevitable. But beyond the Baltic States the picture is much more doubtful.

The big question mark, of course, is Ukraine. No doubt events in that country itself will, more than anything else, determine whether the "new Yalta line" falls to the East or to the West of Ukraine. If the political evolution in Ukraine follows a pattern similar to that in Belarus, few Western countries will contest the development of closer Russo-Ukrainian ties, and Ukraine would then have moved itself behind the 'new Yalta line'.

The Trans-Caucasus area may already be partly behind the new line. Only Azerbaijan is still holding out against Russian pressure to permit basing of forces and control of frontiers and oil. But thus far there has been little interest in the West in giving real support to Azerbaijan, because that would appear to take the Azerbaijani side in the country's bitter dispute with Armenia over the enclave of Nagorno-Karabakh.

The states of Central Asia are already doomed by Western indifference and impotence to be in Russia's new orbit. While technically all these countries can develop relations with the West, there is virtually no chance for them to truly break away from Russia. Western countries have simply been too slow in realizing the significance for the world's economy of the resources of the Caspian basin and Central Asia, which could provide the industrialized nations with fossil fuels well into the next century.

As the Partnership for Peace relationships with NATO are sorted out, they will formalize the 'new Yalta line.' This will not exclude further opportunistic Russian pressures on selected countries, such as Bulgaria or Serbia, which may be more sympathetic and interesting to Russia. It is even possible that, if the ambiguity of the Partnership for Peace period lasts long enough, Russia will succeed in bringing some of the countries of Central and Eastern Europe back under its influence and into its security space. Unfortunately the Partnership for Peace included no barriers to guard against such a possibility.

5. The State of Independence of the Newly Independent States
The situation of each newly-independent state from the former USSR, and the West's response to it, is different. The following brief analysis summarizes the status on a case-by-case basis.

The Baltic States. These three small countries have a history which gives them special consideration, and they have expressed the clearest Western vocation. They have received significant encouragement and assistance from the West, particularly from the Scandinavian countries with which they have a special affinity. Their economies are making progress. Once Russian troops have left Estonia and Latvia, as they are committed to do, independence will be more of a reality. The one remaining problem will be that of the large ethnic Russian minorities, which are resented by the indigenous peoples and could spark difficulties and provide an excuse for Russian intervention later.

Kaliningrad. This area is something of an anomaly because its native population has largely disappeared and it has been made into a huge Russian military base. But it is also clearly a colony and a potentially destabilizing factor. The West has been reluctant to raise the issue, but it has been raised by both Poland and Lithuania and will not go away.

Belarus appears to be headed back toward close association or merger with Russia, and no Western country will contest this.

Moldova is ethnically close to Romania and so has special support from Bucharest. But it also has a complex dispute with ethnic Russians in the Trans-Dniestr region, where a Russian army, with Moscow's encouragement, is defending a breakaway 'republic.' The West has shown little interest in getting involved in this problem.

Ukraine, as mentioned above, is the principal question mark in the area. It is under strong pressure from Russia over debt repayment, fuel supply arrangements, the division of the Black Sea fleet, and perhaps most ominously, the dominant Russian population of Crimea which is seeking a closer relationship with Russia. The West has been keenly interested in Ukraine and its many problems, but has given only half-hearted support. Most Westerners do not want to offend Russia on this issue, and the Ukrainians themselves have been reluctant to follow Western advice on their economy and their nuclear weapons. This is why the question of where Ukraine fits in relation to the 'new Yalta line' will depend primarily on Ukraine itself.

The Trans-Caucasus. Armenia has continued to be heavily dependent on Russia even after its nominal independence, mainly because it needs Russia to offset Turkish support for Azerbaijan in the war over Nagorno-Karabakh. Despite the largely misdirected support of the Armenian diaspora, Armenia appears unlikely to escape the Russian orbit, unless the Karabakh war can be ended very soon. Neither is Georgia after Russia forced its government to accept CIS membership and Russian bases. In a potentially important precedent the UN agreed to monitor the Russian peacekeeping force in Georgia and to set up a fund for voluntary contributions to help pay for it, thus giving it some UN coloration. Since the West was unwilling to provide peacekeepers, this decision sealed Georgia's fate and condemned it to the Russian orbit.

Azerbaijan remains a test case for both Russian intentions and the Western response. It is the one country in the former USSR where there is a valid international offer to monitor a ceasefire in the local conflict. But Russian pressures to accept bases, border guards and oil sharing have been strong, and Azerbaijan has received very little support from the West. It gets better support from Turkey and other Islamic countries, which compounds both Azerbaijan's bitterness and Russia's suspicions.

Central Asia. The key test case in this area thus far has been Tajikistan, where no Western country has been willing to become involved, and where the Russians have installed their troops in support of a friendly regime. Apart from commercial possibilities, such as oil and gas resources, the West is clearly not interested in this area. In fact, many otherwise generous and well-informed

Westerners complain that the newly-independent states of this area were improperly admitted to the Conference on Security and Cooperation in Europe (CSCE), since they are not European. A recent European initiative to look at minority problems went 110 far as to leave this area, as well as the Trans-Caucasus, out entirely, thus signaling that the region is too distant, and its problems too intractible, for Europe to be bothered.

The Russian Federation. The 'empire within an empire' should not be overlooked, despite the West's reluctance to mention it as a potential problem. Within Russia's borders are many colonized areas and people, such as the Tatars, some of which have already raised their voices seeking, and obtaining, greater autonomy. There is of course very little that the West can do in real terms to affect the course of events within the former USSR. At the same time the W oil does have a moral and political responsibility to recognize the situation. there for what they are, and to consider ways in which it can be helpful, even if it is unwilling to become involved on the ground in areas which arc: distant from its central concerns.

6. The Role of the CSCE

But the role of the international community can go beyond just the identification of what is acceptable and what is not. Fortunately, all the new states of the former USSR are members of the CSCE, and so it is possible to use the CSCE in various ways in this area. The CSCE has an excellent record of innovation in the field of preventive diplomacy. Its missions, with mandates tailored to the local circumstances, can be useful and are non-provocative. Such missions could usefully be dispatched for visits, or in some cases, for longer periods, to help to understand problems or ease tensions. The CSCE's High Commissioner for National Minorities and its Office for Democratic Institutions and Human Rights (ODIHR) can also be helpful in these areas. The CSCE is the West's best vehicle for demonstrating concern for these new states, and for providing help in non-provocative ways.

Another worthwhile effort would be to press Russia to negotiate an acceptable basis on which Russian units can participate in

UN or CSCE-sponsored and controlled peacekeeping or monitoring/observing operations on the territory of the former USSR. This will admittedly not be easy, since Russia holds that it has the prerogative to carry out such operations itself, or under the guise of the CIS. Up to now Russia has refused all reasonable proposals for playing such a role under the control of an international organization.

The challenge will be to demonstrate to the Russians, particularly the Russian military, that it is in their interest to share the burdens and responsibilities of these operations with the international community. The Russians do want their operations to be recognized as legitimate by the World Community, and this offers some leverage to international negotiators. More fundamentally, Russia must be brought to understand that if it wishes to be accepted as a responsible member of the World community, it must play by the same rules as apply to other countries. President Boris Yeltsin has a direct responsibility for ensuring that Russia's military leaders, including defense minister Grachev, adhere to these rules.

Up to now, the Western response to Russian policies has been ambiguous, largely because Russia's aims themselves have been ambiguous. But Russia's actions make it increasingly clear that Moscow is determined to regain control over all of the former USSR, with the possible exception of the Baltic States, and that its interventions in the 'near abroad' are important tools for accomplishing this objective. Ultimately the West will have to decide what its attitude will be if and when Russia simply ignores established international standards and pursues its own interests on the territory of the former USSR. And as a part of this process the West will also have to decide whether simply abandoning the new states of this region is compatible with its interests, and its principles.

Annex IV

The End of the Cold War Is Also Over

John J. Maresca

It is popular these days for foreign policy specialists to talk in terms of the "anarchy" or the "chaos" of the post-Cold War world. At the beginning of 1994, Robert Kaplan published a seminal article called "The Coming Anarchy."[1] Madeleine Albright, the U.S. Ambassador to the United Nations, has described the new international Situation as "chaos," and the United States Institute of Peace, the government's think tank for peace studies, made "Managing Chaos" the central theme of its recent tenth-anniversary conference. Citing the world's "chaos" is a way of contrasting the present situation with the simpler "us versus them" equation which the Cold War sustained for 45 years.

But this terminology, though graphic, is misleading. The world is not chaotic, at least no more than it has always been. It is a world in which individual countries are pursuing their varied interests in multiple ways, without much regard for grand unifying themes. In fact, it is the relative stability of the last fifty years that may prove to be a historical aberration.

NATO Is America's European Policy

The foundation of the American foreign policy consensus has now disappeared. That consensus was based on the acceptance by majorities in both American political parties that Communism posed a worldwide threat to American interests, and that this necessitated an active engagement by the United States throughout the world. In particular there was a broad and deep consensus on the need for a strong American commitment to NATO to protect Western Europe from the possibility of Soviet aggression or intimidation.

This Consensus enjoyed remarkable continuity through eight administrations of both Democratic and Republican presidents. A majority of Americans are familiar with NATO, or at least have heard of it, and accept the American commitment to it. There is no other foreign engagement which is so familiar to Americans, and in the two-hundred-year history of the country there has been no foreign commitment to compare with it.

The end of the Cold War, however, changed this. It removed the global threat of Communism and with it the basis for agreement on America's role in the world. NATO has been buffeted by this new and puzzling absence of consensus, as the question of America's future role in Europe has once again been posed.

This raises critical problems because NATO is, or at least has been, Washington's European policy since its inception. It is NATO that defines America's relationship and commitment to Europe; all other aspects of transatlantic relations are peripheral to, or dependent on, this central engagement. Moreover, NATO was a response to a specific threat, emanating from Moscow. NATO has therefore also been at the core of American policy toward the former USSR, now succeeded by Russia.

The New Political Equation

Basic U.S. interests in Europe are the same in 1995 as they have been since the end of the Second World War: peace, stability, democracy, respect for human rights, and economic liberty throughout the continent. But with the collapse of the Communist threat, the political equation within the United States has changed. This is true among both Republicans and Democrats. Within each of these loose political families new groupings have emerged that stress somewhat different foreign policy priorities.

On the right of the political spectrum, there is a split between the "defense-firsters" and the "free-enterprise-firsters". The defense-firsters are still suspicious of Russia. They believe that the potential for a neo-imperialistic Russian nationalism justifies significant defense expenditures and active U.S. engagement overseas. They are prepared to accept some reduction in American defense capabilities, especially in those specific functions which were tailored to the threat of all-out war with the USSR. But they also hope to see new capabilities developed which will respond more directly to local or regional threats, which now appear more likely than global conflict.

Defense-firsters consider preserving NATO's strength independent of Russia essential, because they see Russia as the only potential threat to Europe's security. In their view Russia's military forces, though disorganized and demoralized, are still potentially strong, especially in strategic weapons, submarines, and the raw force of nearly two million men on the territory of the former Soviet Union (FSU). The attack on Chechnya has revealed the military's organizational ineptitude, but also its brute force and determination. The defense-firsters believe that, combined with the uncertainty of Russia's political future, these military forces are still cause for concern, at least in terms of their capacity for intimidation or regional action.

The free-enterprise-firsters believe that the breakup of the USSR has created a unique opportunity to make Russia and its former republics into new bastions of capitalism, and that it is paramount that this conversion occurs as soon as possible. These people are prepared to accept some Russian bravado, such as Moscow's claim to a "sphere of influence", as well as some degree of instability and repression in Russia, while this change takes place. They would like to see America's activities in Russia consist mainly of guarantees for private investment and encouragement of business relations, because they see the advance of a free-enterprise system there as the best way to ensure security.

The free-enterprise-firsters are also partly neo-isolationists. They see no need for U.S. forces to be engaged in distant places anymore; and would prefer that America be involved only when essential U.S. interests are clearly at risk. Their tests for judging 'essential U.S. interests,' tend to be economic. Thus, these people supported American intervention in Kuwait, but not in Haiti, Somalia, or Rwanda. They also tend to believe it is time for Europeans to take care of their own problems, or at least to pay for their own security, and see a far reduced need for American engagement on the European continent. These attitudes reinforce each other to produce strong resistance to U.S. engagement in the former Yugoslavia or the former USSR.

On the left of the spectrum, too, there are confusing new divisions that mirror those on the right. Many opposed American military interventions overseas during the Cold War because they felt American lives were being risked unnecessarily in areas where America's interests were limited, and because these interventions seemed to put the United States on the side of dictators who were oppressing their people or stifling the democratic process. Now, these same people find themselves favoring U.S. interventions on humanitarian grounds in places like Haiti or Rwanda. Bosnia is a dilemma for them, clearly a humanitarian problem, but one that would be better handled by Europeans. Although they would like to see a new focus for U.S. military forces, they tend to favor American engagement overseas.

But the left also has its neo-isolationists. These are the people who believe that America has enough problems of its own, and that the U.S. should concentrate the nation's political energies at home, on the growing challenges of crime, violence, drugs, and homelessness, among others. It was this group that was the key to the election of Bill Clinton, "the domestic policy president" who had no experience whatsoever in foreign affairs, over George Bush, the victor of the Gulf War, former Ambassador to the UN and former director of the CIA.

The new divisions in both halves of the American political spectrum have prevented the formation of a new consensus on America's role in the post-Cold War world. Even those who favor an active overseas role differ on what its objectives should be. The result has been indecision, as in the case of Bosnia; confusion over objectives, as in Somalia or in the debate over the proper response to Chechnya; and procrastination, exemplified by the Partnership for Peace approach to the question of NATO expansion. This failure is not simply one of the Clinton administration. It began, in fact, during the final two years of the Bush presidency, and would probably have haunted George Bush had he been reelected. Rather, it reflects a major, if so far largely unfocused, national debate about the role the United States should play in the post-Cold War world.

A firm bipartisan American foreign policy could reemerge if a major new threat to American interests appeared. This is not out of the question; an anti-Western and aggressively nationalist regime in Moscow, for example, would constitute such a threat, and could revive broadly felt fears of the Russians. Or another Iraq, perhaps armed with nuclear weapons, could emerge. But neither of these prospects seems likely in the immediate future, at least not in the stark terms which would be required to provoke a decisive change in American policy (although Chechnya could signal a start in this direction). In fact, we are more likely to see threats which resemble Bosnia—local, confusing, largely civil, and in which it is difficult to differentiate the "good guys" from the bad. Such conflicts actually detract attention from the broader issue of defining new goals for America's foreign policy.

Descriptions of the new geopolitical Situation as "chaos" or "anarchy" reflect the frustration of intellectuals faced with this new situation, and an avoidance of their responsibility to provide coherent analyses of events. Such a perception also fuels arguments on both the left and the right for an American withdrawal from the world. These images are in any case wrong, for the developments we are seeing in the former USSR, former Yugoslavia, the Islamic world, and elsewhere have their explanations and their logic, as complex and unfamiliar they may be to the West.

The End of the Cold War Is Over

Just as the Cold War is over, the period known as "the end of the Cold War" is also over. That brief phase was one of optimism that East and West would finally be united, and would work together to construct a stable and prosperous Europe. Unfortunately, this hope faded rapidly.

The turnabout began in late 1992 or the beginning of 1993, as Russia appeared to turn toward authoritarianism, aggressive nationalism, and an imperialistic foreign policy. The first signal of this change came in Foreign Minister Andrei Kozyrevs "mock speech" at the ministerial session of the CSCE in Stockholm in December of 1992. Kozyrev's aggressive, hard-line speech shocked his listeners. His comments with respect to the "near abroad"[2] were particularly harsh; Kozyrev asserted that "The space of the former Soviet Union cannot be viewed as a zone where the CSCE norms can be applied in full. This is in effect a post-imperial space where Russia has to defend its interests by all available means, including military and economic ones. We shall firmly insist that the former republics of the USSR immediately join the new federation or confederation, and this will be discussed in no uncertain terms."[3]

An hour later, possibly because journalists were sending off dramatic reports of the event, Kozyrev took the floor again to explain that it was a hoax. He claimed that he just wanted to warn his colleagues of what Russia's policies might be like if hard-line nationalists gained power.

Yet the policies of the Yeltsin government evolved rapidly from that time, especially on a few leading-edge issues such as the role of the international community in resolving the Nagorno-Karabakh war. Before 1993 was over Kozyrev's "real" policies closely resembled the hard-line nationalist policies of his "mock" Stockholm speech. In particular, Russia's determination to regain control over as much as possible of the former USSR had become obvious to all but the most naive Western observers.[4]

Some analysts have suggested that the Yeltsin government adjusted its policies because of the electoral strength shown by Vladimir Zhirinovsky, a virulent nationalist, in the Russian parliamentary elections in the autumn of 1993. While this made the world conscious of the nationalist trend in Russia, in fact the evolution of policy began much earlier. The appearance of Zhirinovsky merely revealed the growing depth and breadth of nationalist feeling as Russia progressed through a period of economic and political retrenchment.

The general state of disarray in Moscow makes it difficult to find an authoritative statement of Russian foreign policy, particularly in the critical area of the newly independent states of the former USSR. There may be no centrally developed or approved policy concept or policy objectives. Rather, foreign policy may reflect an accumulation of separate actions by different ministries, all seeking to anticipate what they see as the tendency of political opinion.

But by observing Russian actions, and the aims which Russian negotiators have pursued in their dealings with the new states, it is possible to draw up a tentative list of policy directions. Based on this crude revival of Kremlinology, the Russians appear to want:

- Control of the outer frontiers of the whole of the former USSR. The Russians point out that there were no marked or even surveyed internal borders in the former USSR, and to establish them now would be very costly.[5] By their logic, a better solution is simply to reestablish the old frontiers, and man them with Russian border forces. Current exceptions to this general rule include the Baltic States and Azerbaijan, but in the latter case the Russians are actively pressing for reintroduction of their border guards along the frontier with Iran.

- To maintain military bases throughout the former USSR. After the Russians forced Eduard Shevardnadze to capitulate and invite Russian forces into Georgia, and after Russia's troops finally agreed to leave the Baltic states of Estonia and Latvia, Russian basing rights are in question only in Azerbaijan, where the government clearly does not want the Russians to return and is resisting strong pressure to agree to the reopening of their large base in Gandzha. The other new states never managed to get rid of the Russians.

- Control of natural resources throughout the former USSR, particularly energy resources. Not only does Russia itself need these resources, it also knows that they are a prime source of hard currency, and could enable some former colonies to escape from Russian control. The Russian technique for gaining control over resources is not very subtle: Russia simply demands a share, and insists that

pipeline routes from the Caucasus and Central Asia
should cross Russia.

- To keep the international community out. This means in
  particular the United States and its surrogates. Russian
  xenophobes are determined to exclude both American influence and Turkish or Islamic influences, to which Russia
  is particularly sensitive along its southern frontier.
- Finally, the Russians are determined to prevent a breakup
  of the Russian Federation itself, the "empire within an
  empire," which includes many colonized peoples. The favored technique for ensuring control over Russia is to
  reestablish control over the whole of the former USSR
  through consolidation of the Russian-dominated Commonwealth of Independent States (CIS). This would
  reestablish the traditional buffer zones and theoretically
  insulate the Russian Federation from such potential instabilities.

All of these neo-imperialist policies have been clearly displayed in
Russia's brutal attack on Chechnya. It is of course technically true
that Chechnya lies within the borders of the Russian Federation as
they are recognized by every other country in the world. But the
offensive against Grozny has raised many issues which transcend
frontiers, such as the international obligation of all governments to
respect the human rights of their citizens. And in the course of the
attack Russia has broken its engagements in numerous treaties,
including the Treaty on Conventional Forces in Europe {CFE} and
the Charter of the United Nations, the Helsinki Final Act, the
Charter of Paris for a New Europe, the Agreement on Confidence
and Security-Building Measures (CSBMs), and the Summit Document of the Budapest Meeting of the OSCE. Less than two weeks
before ordering the attack on Chechnya Yeltsin himself signed the
OSCE Code of Conduct covering, inter alia, how a state deals with
internal conflicts.

Violating treaty obligations and other international undertakings is a fundamentally international matter not an "internal" affair. The extraordinary demonstration by Yeltsin's government of
neo-imperialism, of dictatorial repression, of brutal disregard for

human rights, and of disdain for public opinion in Russia and the world puts the Yeltsin government in the same category as the Soviet regimes of the past. In short, the period known as the "end of the Cold War" has been resoundingly concluded by Russia's attack on Grozny. It is simply no longer possible to speak of a "democratic" government in the Kremlin; democratic governments do not attempt crudely to destroy cities and whole peoples on their own territory. On the contrary, democratic governments are under heavy international obligations to protect their own citizens and their rights. Those in the West who are fond of arguing that unless the West supports Yeltsin it will be faced with "a worse alternative" must face up to the fact that Yeltsin himself is responsible for Grozny; that for the Chechens there is very little that could be "worse"; and that the only domestic support for this lunatic venture has come from Vladimir Zhirinovsky himself, everyone's nominal "worse alternative."

The West, particularly the United States, must now develop a much more realistic analysis of Russia and the world as it is in 1995, and as it is likely to evolve into the next century. Such an analysis must form the basis for a new American foreign policy consensus and a coherent, clear and consistent U.S. role in the world. More than anything else, the world needs steady leadership in this rapidly changing period. This leadership must be based on firm moral values and political direction, and only America can provide it.

It is against this background that the question of America's future role in European security, and in relation to Russia, must be viewed. This debate may not reach a conclusion for a number of years, but its parameters are nonetheless instructive. The principal issues on which this discussion is currently focused are:

- U.S. and Western relations with Russia, and Russia's future role.
- NATO's possible expansion to the east.
- U.S. and international "peacekeeping" interventions.
- The level and roles of U.S. forces in Europe.

Each of these issues entails aspects of the broader question of America's international role, but each also reflects other factors, both internal to the United States and broadly international. Same may be affected over the next two years by the semi-lame-duck status of President Clinton as he faces a Republican-controlled Congress. But primarily these issues are being debated on their merits, whether they be domestic or foreign.

Relations With Russia, and Russia's Role

Washington has always believed that it has a special relationship with Moscow. This was true during the Second World War, when the United States and the USSR formed the essential partnership for victory; it was true during the Cold War, as the fundamental world security equation was based on the rough equilibrium between Soviet and American strategic forces; and it remains true in the post-Cold War period. America continues to, have special responsibilities in the effort to bring Russia into a constructive relationship with the West, for example by enduring adherence to the obligations of their treaties on strategic nuclear weapons.

The primacy of the relationship with Russia, and particularly of the need to ensure responsible control over the former nuclear arsenal, has affected all aspects of American thinking and policy since the end of the Cold War. It led immediately to U.S. acceptance of Russia as the principal successor state to the USSR without much thought as to the implications of this step for the other newly independent states of the Soviet Union. It also led to the creation in the U.S. State Department of a specific bureau for the former Soviet Union, headed by that well-known "Friend of Bill" (Clinton), Strobe Talbott.[6]

This separation of the former Soviet area from its previous bureaucratic lodgings in the Bureau of European Affairs inevitably made Russia the primary policy consideration for the key foreign affairs official of the new administration. Previously, Russian needs had been offset in the policy process by other European needs-those of NATO, the European Union, or major allies like Germany. But in the Clinton administration responsibility for

American policy toward Russia was given to the dynamic and well-connected Talbott, while European policy was tended separately by the inexperienced and unknown Stephen Oxman, who has since been replaced.

Russia's primacy in the American policy process also led to the creation of the NATO Partnership for Peace program, discussed below, as well as Washington's growing implicit acceptance of Russia's claim to a "sphere of influence" on the territory of the former Soviet Union, with the possible exception of the Baltic States. What Washington has failed to understand or take into account is that the former USSR is currently going through an anticolonial struggle similar to those which in the past have preceded the disintegration of empires, with far-reaching implications.

When the rotting structure of an empire begins to crumble, the process of breakup follows a predictable pattern. Neither the colonial populations nor the people of the mother country are prepared, politically or psychologically, for the separation, and the result is a protracted period of struggle. This provokes violence in the colonial areas, and a mass exodus back to the mother country. Economic chaos tends to be pervasive, and bitterness in the mother country leads to nationalistic rear-guard actions aimed at preventing or reversing the colonies' progress toward independence. In the colonized areas the struggle is often fratricidal as a new national identity is forged, political alliances are formed or broken, and minority groups within a colony sometimes try to capitalize on the moment to seize their own freedom.

In most cases, this period of struggle has preceded the independence of the colonies, with some spillover into the post-independence period. The Russian/Soviet empire was not immune to these symptoms. But instead of experiencing this period of struggle primarily before the colonies achieved independence, in the Russian case it is happening largely after their nominal independence. In fact, Russia and its former empire the so-called "near abroad" are going through this struggle now, and will probably take years, possibly decades, to complete the transition. All of the features of exodus, bitterness, economic chaos, rear-guard actions, and fratricidal competition have appeared in parts of the FSU, and will surely emerge elsewhere before the process has run its course.

In Moscow political leaders are wrestling with the problems posed by this period of decolonization. Ironically, the situation parallels in many ways the circumstances which followed the Bolshevik revolution, when many areas which had been colonized by the czars also broke away from Russia and enjoyed brief periods of independence. The Bolsheviks used a variety of techniques to regain control over the breakaway republics, just as Moscow is doing now in an effort to resist their further movement toward real independence.

There is little agreement in Moscow as to how to retain the "empire," or even whether this is a good idea. Although millions of Russians believe it was a mistake to let the near abroad go, many Russians are also aware that restoring Russia's dominance over these former colonies will also restore Russia's responsibility for them. Each one of them is besieged by complex problems, and the Russian government is already struggling just to keep Russia itself united and economically viable.

But as often happens in periods of difficulty, aggressive nationalism appears to be winning the debate over the proper role for Russia in the near abroad. As a consequence, there has been no objection to the fact that the defense ministry has taken the lead in formulating Russia's policies in the FSU, ostensibly with the purpose of restoring order and ensuring security on Russia's frontiers.

The Russian defense establishment has been an armed force without a mission since the collapse of Communism, which formed its ideological justification and gave it a purpose. Now it is being positioned, politically and psychologically, to be the defender of the ethnic Russian populations in the newly independent states, and the guarantor of stability everywhere on the territory of the former Soviet Union. This mission may help to give the Russian army a new sense of purpose.

The world's image of the Russian armed forces is of a demoralized, underfunded, ill-housed, and unprepared military organization which is no longer a threat to international security.

This may be true at the global level, with the important caveat of Russia's nuclear arsenal. But on the territory of the former USSR the Russian army still looms large. Russia's armed forces have almost two million men under arms, the full range of equipment, and a tough approach to problems which is often reflected in the comments of their leader, Defense Minister Pavel Grachev. Despite the problems encountered in the attack on Grozny, this is a military force which is capable of intervening anywhere in the former USSR, and which has already done so with relative success in Tajikistan, Georgia, and Moldova.

The Russian army has interlinked bases, command, control and communications channels, and supply routes throughout ex-Soviet territory. It controls mountains of weapons and ammunition supplies, plus "volunteers" and cheap mercenaries of every technical specialty. Its officer corps, primarily Slavic, is a far-flung fraternity that still has enormous influence in every defense ministry in the newly independent states. Furthermore, the old KGB intelligence and internal security networks are still largely intact, and very little can happen in the vast ex-Soviet space without it being known in the defense and internal security ministries in Moscow.

The development of the CIS has helped to provide a facade of international cooperation toward dealing with conflicts within the former USSR. Russia has also tried to obtain international acceptance of the CIS as an organization equivalent to, say, the European Union. It has argued that the CIS has exclusive competence for dealing with conflicts on the territory of the former USSR. In cases which have elicited international interest, such as Georgia, Azerbaijan, and Tajikistan, the Russians have made a point of calling their proposed peacekeeping interventions CIS operations, even when participation by non-Russian CIS members was no more than symbolic. All CIS operations would, of course, be dominated or possibly even exclusively manned by Russia.

Russian suspicions of outside attempts to settle problems in the former USSR have been manifested most strongly in the behavior of Russian representatives with regard to the conflict over the mountain enclave of Nagorno-Karabakh, in the Trans-

Caucasus, because this is the one conflict on former Soviet territory in which an international body—the "Minsk Group"—has been mandated to find a solution. Here the Russians, led by Defense Minister Grachev, have made a concerted effort to undercut international initiatives, to keep the international community out, and to resolve the problem themselves, using their own troops, as a way of ensuring their domination of the region. The Russians have appeared prepared to accept accusations of bad faith in this instance, as the price of ensuring exclusive Russian predominance.[8]

Because of the confusion of attitudes toward foreign engagements which has followed the end of the Cold War, there has up to now been no concerted challenge to the "Russia first" policy of the Clinton administration, even in response to the deeply disturbing moral issues raised by the war on the Chechens. But such a challenge is likely to grow, for several reasons:

- There is a rising perception in the United States that Russia is moving away from the cooperative foreign policy of the first Yeltsin years, and toward a posture of more open and problematic competition with the West. This new Russian attitude has emerged to contest Western, primarily American, policies in the Middle East, Iraq, Iran, Korea, and the former Yugoslavia, among other areas.
- Russia's heavy-handed efforts to reestablish its dominance of the countries of the former Soviet Union have alarmed some Americans. Russian behavior in Georgia and Azerbaijan, for example, has suggested to many observers that the KGB and its old methods are not dead. The attack on Grozny, though technically "internal" to Russia, has reinforced this impression.
- Russian arms sales or other close associations with pariah states such as Serbia—Iran, and Iraq have suggested the potential for renewed worldwide confrontation. Russia's apparent interest in gaining a zone of influence extending to the Persian Gulf and including Azerbaijan, Iran, and Iraq is particularly worrying.

- The return of former Communist apparatchiks to political power or other positions of influence in Moscow and throughout the former Communist countries has caused concern among American observers of the area.
- Finally, Russian actions in Chechnya have revealed all of the above factors and have made them a subject of broad discussion in the West. These actions have underscored the brutal, undemocratic nature of the Russian government and its methods, and launched a wave of popular revulsion toward Russia.
- These developments have strengthened the arguments of those Americans who believe that Russia is still a potential security threat, especially to the newly independent states, of the former USSR, but also to the countries of Eastern and Central Europe. There has been a revival of interest in preserving NATO's independence from Russian influence, and in responding to the security concerns of the' Central and East Europeans. Interest in finding a way to bring them into a closer association with NATO is growing, even among the Russia-firsters of the Clinton administration.

The debate over Russia's role is not over yet. President Clinton has protested Russian pressures on Azerbaijan directly to Boris Yeltsin,[9] and the international community has roused itself at least to the extent of offering a multinational CSCE peacekeeping force as an alternative to deployment of unwanted Russian army units in Azerbaijan to supervise the cease-fire in the conflict over Nagorno-Karabakh.[10] Whether the CSCE member-states will actually be able to deliver on this offer, or whether the Russians will overtly — or covertly — sabotage the effort, remains to be seen.

NATO Expansion

Perhaps the most real and symbolic problem posed by the Cold War's end is finding a means to provide security for those countries which were formerly members of the Warsaw Pact, following the withdrawal of the Soviet army from their territories. In the first instance this concerns Poland, the Czech Republic, and Hungary, but also Slovakia, Romania, and Bulgaria, the Baltic States, and possibly Slovenia and Albania as well. Some would argue that it also relates to Ukraine, Moldova, and eventually other post-Yugoslav states, though those states pose more difficult issues.

These countries are all currently in a security vacuum of some kind, and are increasingly uneasy about their non-membership in any larger security grouping. Poland, the Czech Republic, and Hungary are obvious test cases, because of their proximity to the West, their comparatively rapid pace of post-Communist reform, and their ability to develop political sympathies in the West. All three of these countries have indicated that they wish to become NATO members, while Russia has made clear that any expansion of NATO to the east would be considered an unfriendly act with negative implications for Russia's own security.

The response of the Clinton administration to this quandary was to initiate NATO's so-called "Partnership for Peace" program, under which any non-NATO country in Europe or the former Soviet Union can develop a bilateral relationship with NATO. The idea was to mollify the Central Europeans, while easing Russian concerns by giving Moscow (at least potentially) equal access to the Western Alliance. Over time, it was hoped, some countries (i.e., Poland) would naturally grow closer to NATO, which would justify early membership, while others (Russia) would remain more distant and would then be more prepared to accept a NATO expansion which did not include them.

The weakness of the Partnership for Peace program is that it gives all the countries of Europe and the former USSR the same potential relationship with NATO. Austria or Poland theoretically has the same likelihood of developing a close relationship with, or joining, NATO as does Kyrgyzstan or Tajikistan, or even Russia itself. This is clearly absurd, and the net effect of the Partnership for Peace program has been to postpone the difficult decisions about which countries would be close to, or join, NATO, and fall on the Western side of a "new Yalta line," and which countries would not develop such close relations, and would find themselves on the Eastern side of the line. Since Russia itself cannot join NATO without destroying it or at least rendering it meaningless, the Eastern side of the new line will by default be a Russian-dominated area.

The Partnership for Peace thus reinforced the security vacuum in which the countries of Central and Eastern Europe wait. The resulting sense of doubt and uncertainty, far from the Partnership's stated purpose of creating a Europe without dividing lines, actually adds to the instability of the present situation. Moreover, it tempts Russian nationalists to reassert themselves in these places too.

Of the states of the former USSR, the Baltic States have been clearest in stating that they want to become a part of the West. Given their special history and Western outlook, they will probably continue to receive strong Western support. Even the Russians appear to have accepted this as inevitable by agreeing to withdraw their forces from the area.

Beyond the Baltic States the picture is much more doubtful, particularly with regard to Ukraine. More than anything else, internal events in Ukraine will determine whether the "new Yalta line" falls east or west of it. If Ukraine's political evolution follows a pattern similar to that in Belarus, few Western countries will contest the development of closer Russo-Ukrainian ties, and Ukraine would then have moved itself east of the new Yalta line.

The Trans-Caucasus area may already be behind the new line. Only Azerbaijan is still holding out against Russian pressure to permit basing of forces and control over frontiers and oil. But thus far the West has shown little interest in giving significant support to Azerbaijan, for fear of appearing to take the Azerbaijani side in the country's bitter dispute with Armenia over the enclave of Nagorno-Karabakh.

The states of Central Asia already appear doomed by Western indifference and impotence to stay in Russia's new orbit. While technically these countries can develop relations with the West, they have virtually no chance to truly break away from Russia. Western countries failed to realize the significance of the resources of the Caspian basin and Central Asia for the world's economy: they could provide the industrialized nations with fossil fuels well into the next century.

As the Partnership for Peace relationships with NATO are sorted out, the new Yalta line will be formalized. This will not exclude further opportunistic Russian pressures on selected countries) such as Bulgaria or Serbia, which may be more sympathetic and interesting to Russia. It is even possible that, if the ambiguity of the Partnership for Peace period lasts long enough, Russia will succeed in bringing some of the countries of Central and Eastern Europe back under its influence and into its security space. The Partnership for Peace included no barriers to guard against such a possibility.

Unfortunately, the hoped for positive effects of the Partnership for Peace have not emerged. The Central Europeans are increasingly adrift, possibly even slipping back toward the East. Russia is even more hostile to NATO expansion than it was two years ago, when at least there was some ambiguity in Moscow's position. It is now apparent that the "Partnership" was really a form of procrastination on this difficult issue, and the somewhat sparse early objections to it are gaining ground. Increasingly, pundits have noted that the "Partnership" absurdly equates the relationship of Poland to NATO, for example, with that of Uzbekistan to NATO. Analysts also point out the irrationality of trying to reassure the Central Europeans on their principal security concern-Russia-by offering to bring Russia into a close relationship with NATO.[11]

The procrastination effect of the Partnership for Peace program has polarized the American debate between those who consider it important to include as many Central and East European countries as possible in NATO, as early as possible, and those who think it more important not to provoke Russia, or who simply question the wisdom of extending the American nuclear umbrella over any additional countries.

The issue is not a simple one. Any extension of NATO would require ratification by the Senate, because it would be a major amendment to the North Atlantic Treaty. In view of the U.S. commitment to help defend the territory of the NATO member-states, through use of American nuclear weapons if necessary, such a step would entail a major debate. It is not at all certain that the Senate would ratify an expansion of NATO, especially in a situation where an unpopular Democratic president must deal with an aroused, Republican-controlled Senate. The presence of the ultraconservative Senator Jesse Helms as chairman of the Senate Foreign Relations Committee would not help. Many observers in Washington believe in the interest of achieving a solution. That, of course is precisely what is required for true peacekeeping efforts where backing either side is excluded.

Peacekeeping requires legitimacy and impartiality as well as the ability to carry out whatever operations are necessary. In the modern world the key component — legitimacy — can only be provided by an international organization with recognized authority and impartiality. The United Nations is the principal legitimizer of peacekeeping Operations, but in the case of Europe and the former Soviet Union it is also possible that the Organization for Security and Cooperation in Europe (OSCE) could fill this role. The use of force by peacekeeping units, however, can only be authorized by the UN Security Council, under Chapter VII of the Charter of the United Nations.

But Americans are uncomfortable working with the United Nations. This discomfort is acute with the current secretary general, since many Americans suspect him of seeking his own independent military capability. Any U.S. administration will be extremely reluctant to put American troops under international command. At the same time, America's participation in and support of international peacekeeping is essential. It begins in the Security Council (or the OSCE) itself, where American opposition can prevent agreement on an intervention. Also, it is true in the practical dimension: only the United States has the logistics capability to support a large operation in a distant part of the globe. And American support is virtually a sine qua non for some aspects of peacekeeping operations: financing for countries which cannot pay for the participation of their own troops, intelligence and communications; for forces in the field, and the military muscle and reach to protect a peacekeeping force if that should become necessary.

In many ways the operation in Haiti, optimistically codenamed "Restore Democracy," was ideal for the United States. It was given a mandate by the Security Council and therefore was legitimate. It was nearby, and it could be justified in terms of right and wrong. It also appeared likely to ease a key domestic political problem for the United States—the large numbers of desperately poor (and black) boat people who were fleeing the Haitian regime and seeking illegal entry into an America increasingly resistant to immigration. Furthermore, the possibility of American casualties was low. The real problem, which remains, was how to get out once there.

But America's political need to do something about Haiti may have led to a tacit acquiescence to the Yalta-like concept of "sphere-of-influence peacekeeping." This would delegate to each power the responsibility for peacekeeping "in its own backyard": most obviously the United States in the Americas, the European Union (EU) in Europe—and Russia in the Commonwealth of Independent States. This reasoning assumes that Russia is now a democratic state like any other and can be counted on to handle peacekeeping operations responsibly, and that the EU is capable of joint security operations.

The problem is that neither of these assumptions is correct. In Russia's case, the Chechnya venture has starkly confirmed that Russia is not a democracy, at least not yet, and its relationship with the other newly independent states of the CIS remains very much one of a colonial master to its colonies. The contrast with America's approach to Haiti is stark: for Americans the principal consideration is how to get out as quickly as possible; for Russia the problem is how to arrange the dependency of its neighboring states so that Russia's dominance, and the Russian presence, will be permanent.

The Russian military and its backers label all their operations in the near abroad "peacekeeping," and believe that their operations should be supported and even paid for by the broader international community. But the Russian concept of peacekeeping is quite different from the classic definition, and contrasts sharply not only with the long-standing practices of the United Nations in this field, but also with normal relations among independent states.

The Russian concept of "peacekeeping" looks like forceful suppression of violence, rather than the impartial and pacific approach of international organizations. Even the expression, in Russian, means something different. Russian troops engaged in such operations are authorized to use force not only to defend themselves if they are attacked, but also to suppress violations of the peace, whatever the cause. UN peacekeeping missions are only authorized to use force in self-defense.

Russian "peacekeeping" also does not promote the negotiation of stable political solutions as is the case in international Operations. Suppression of violence is itself the goal. For the international-community peacekeeping is an unavoidable expedient which may make it possible to organize negotiations aimed at resolving the underlying dispute. In this approach the goal is clearly the achievement of a negotiated political solution, not just the suppression of violence.

The Russian approach grows naturally out of the historical experience of the Russian and Soviet armed forces in handling security problems within the USSR. When such problems arose, the army was sent to impose order. It often accomplished this objective brutally, and in some cases the legacy the army left behind only complicated or intensified the underlying dispute. Many historians contend that in fact Stalin deliberately kept local hostilities alive, or even created them, in order to ensure that distant parts of the Soviet Union would always be dependent on the center for their security.[15] This raises the prospect that Russian "peacekeeping" troops would use intimidation or force to suppress elements they considered unfavorable to Moscow's interests, just as Soviet forces did before them.

Coupled with this interpretation of their "peacekeeping" role, the Russians feel strongly that maintaining peace and stability on the terr1tory of the former OSSR remains their exclusive prerogative. This, too, resembles the possessive attitudes of virtually all colonial powers with respect to their former colonies. But it is perhaps felt even more strongly in Russia because of the country's historic xenophobia. Many Russians see their country as having a unique role throughout Eurasia, and do not believe Outsiders have any place in this region.

As for the European Union, the Yugoslav experience has revealed the real limits of its current ability to carry out joint foreign policy activities. Nonetheless, the American political class concurs that Europeans should be doing more to take care of their own security problems. This is consistent with the American stress on the need for "burdensharing" — getting 'the Europeans to spend more on defense, and to pay more in support of American forces stationed in Europe — which was a constant American theme during the Cold War.

America' natural inclination to expect Europeans to do more for their own security was reinforced by the Maastricht Treaty and its undertaking to "define and implement a common foreign and security policy."[16] When Yugoslavia began to break up, these two factors led Washington to push the European Union into the lead position in dealing with this complex crisis.[17] Additionally, the Bush administration was basking in the glory of its victory in the Gulf War, and did not wish to risk tarnishing that success with the possibility of a less positive outcome in Yugoslavia. Unfortunately, Europe was unable to contain this conflict, which was subsumed by the United Nations.

The Yugoslav experience is instructive in many ways. First, it has demonstrated the need for the international community to apply more preventive activities, earlier in pre-conflict situations. Second, the Bosnian war showed that NATO is unable to respond to certain military challenges. This was the first instance in which NATO was used as an organization for applying military force under mandate from the United Nations, and although there have been recurrent problems relating to decision-making authority and multiple chains-of-command in Bosnia, this could be a useful model for the future. It shows how a peacekeeping operation can be mandated by the UN, and yet make use of the operational capacities of the United States through its role in NATO. Nonetheless, the stark reality of the alliance's inability to respond in military terms remains.

It would be useful if NATO could acquire a new role in peacekeeping operations, both because it would mark out a new post-Cold War function for the military alliance, and because it would be a way to involve the United States in responses to the kinds of localized conflicts which appear more likely in the corning years than an all-out East-West military confrontation. Washington may be more willing to place its forces under UN command if it is part of a UN-mandated NATO operation. One can assume that this would also be true of a CSCE-mandated NATO operation, if there should ever be agreement on such an arrangement. But it is clear that without a mandate from a more broadly based international organization, NATO can have no role in peacekeeping.

What about Russian peacekeeping in the CIS? This poses a problem for Americans at the moment, especially in light of the conflict in Chechnya. It also forms part of the larger debate over Russia's future role. Those who are uneasy about Russia's political future and believe that the West must maintain its defense capabilities against the possible rebirth of an aggressive Russian security threat, think Russia's actions in Chechnya and the newly independent countries of the former USSR already reflect neoimperialistic tendencies. The Russian attack on Chechnya, even though it was within the borders of the Russian Federation, was a watershed that confirmed their worst fears. Those who are concerned with the military balance and Russia's "order of battle" are particularly uneasy about Russia's evident violations of its obligations under the Treaty on Conventional Forces in Europe (CFE) and the Agreement on Confidence and Security-Building Measures (CSBMs) as the Chechnya attack was carried out. These violations reflect Russia's stated objective of moving more heavy weapons — tanks artillery, and armored personnel carriers — into its so-called "flank" areas, principally the northern Caucasus.

To others, acceptance of "sphere-of-influence peacekeeping" appears both logical and advantageous. These people argue that despite the brutality, Chechnya is an "internal" Russian matter;

moreover, no other country or organization is likely to undertake peace-keeping responsibilities on the territory of the former USSR. Certainly the United States, with all its hesitations about becoming involved in the war in Bosnia, will not put forces in the CIS, and NATO cannot be used there. The choice in the CIS, then, is between peacekeeping by Russia or no peacekeeping at all. The Americans who argue this logic do not believe Russia is interested in, or capable of, reestablishing full control over the newly independent countries, and that a Russian-sponsored stability is better than none.[18]

The current test case for Russia's role in the near abroad is whether the peacekeeping force which will supervise the cease-fire in the long and bloody conflict over Nagorno-Karabakh will be a Russian/CIS force or a multinational CSCE force. For the last two years, Russia has been trying to undercut the international effort and keep a CSCE force out of the area. This suggests that Moscow is not simply interested in helping to end the war, but is using the situation to move its army back into Azerbaijan, from which it was obliged to withdraw in 1992.[19]

Russia's "sphere of influence" is likely to be defined by the area in which its "peacekeeping" activities are considered legitimate, or at least are not contested. This clearly has more far-reaching implications than the peacekeeping operations alone. The Russian "sphere of influence," once established and widely accepted, will form the de facto new Yalta line, and will be difficult to change thereafter. Those countries which have the misfortune to fall on the eastern side of this line will be condemned to a situation of limited sovereignty for many years to come.

A few Americans have expressed alarm because of Russia's dubious conduct in Georgia and Azerbaijan.[20] But others have shrugged their shoulders and are inclined to espouse the "sphere-of-influence peacekeeping" approach tacitly accepted by President Clinton himself when he announced the deployment of American troops to Haiti in the fall of 1994. The neo-isolationists recoil at the idea of any engagement on the territory of the former USSR. Even those who favor new forms of humanitarian and peacekeeping intervention hesitate before the difficulties of such activities in areas of Russian dominance. In addition, there is a widely accepted belief that outside interventions in the former USSR would risk provoking a nationalistic Russian reaction.

Moreover, it is dear that Russia has special interests in the former USSR, and is now working to reunite this vast territory through the CIS. Just what the CIS is remains unclear.

Is it, as the Russians claim, a "regional organization" as established by the terms of the UN Charter, and thus a legitimate institution for undertaking peacekeeping interventions? Or is it a neocolonial structure which serves as an instrument for reestablishing or maintaining Russia's control over its former empire?

The answer lies in Russia's total domination of the CIS. The CIS is not based on the equal sovereignty of its member-states, but on the universal primacy of one state-Russia. Because the other members have a lesser, and therefore limited, sovereignty, the organization is incompatible with the principles of the Charter. The CIS cannot have legitimate responsibility for peacekeeping interventions for this reason; it simply is not a free association of equally sovereign states.

While no Western leader would admit to being prepared to accept a new Yalta-type division of Europe, no one, in Washington or in Europe, seems inclined to do anything about this looming development. Many, in fact, especially in Europe, appear to favor writing off the Caucasus and Central Asia anyway, on the grounds that they "are not European."

Unfortunately, the Bosnian experience is likely to remain as a point of reference for American policymakers considering any future U.S. involvement in peacekeeping operations in Europe. Europe's perceived inability to muster the political will to enforce a peaceful settlement is likely to discourage American leaders from joining such undertakings, since they will not want to become responsible for European security problems about which the Europeans themselves appear to be indecisive or indifferent.

Levels of Roles of U.S. Forces in Europe

In the last five years the level of U.S. military personnel in Europe has fallen rapidly from about 250,000 to about 100,000. Many of the troops who were sent to Saudi Arabia for the Gulf War simply never returned to their bases in Germany, but were withdrawn directly to the United States. A number of American installations have been closed as a part of this drawdown, notably the militarily useless but highly symbolic American garrison in Berlin, withdrawn along with its Russian, British, and French Counterparts. The overall change is dramatic, in keeping with the significance of the Cold War's end.

The number of American troops in Europe has for years been regarded as a barometer of American commitment; whenever there were political pressures to reduce this number, Europeans saw this as evidence of weakening U.S. interest in West European security. When U.S. forces were transferred elsewhere, as during the Vietnam War, Europeans were convinced that American priorities had shifted to other regions. The most remarkable aspect of this long American presence, however, was its basic consistency in spite of all the fluctuations, with troop levels averaging between 250,000 and 300,000 for several decades.

There was never a precise analytical basis for the numbers of U.S. troops in Europe, though there were many attempts over the years to establish one. In the end such studies wound up justifying previously conceived notions of the most effective force levels. For many years 300,000 troops seemed to be accepted as the correct force presence, both for its effectiveness and its symbolism. But toward the end of the Cold War numerous studies and articles tried to rationalize lower figures. During the same period the U.S. Army refined the technique of leaving equipment in place for use by a returning army, used most recently in Kuwait. Use of this technique tended to increase the effectiveness of lower force levels.

For the last few years the figure of 100,000 has been widely accepted as the proper level of troops, both symbolically and militarily, to ensure European confidence in American support for European security. But with the "soviet threat" having disappeared, and greater political attention to domestic problems, some Americans have advocated lower troop levels, such as 60,000 or even 50,000. In response, military planners have argued that 60,000 is the lowest level at which an army can effectively defend itself, and that it would not be acceptable in military terms to reduce U.S. forces in Europe below that figure. There is also continuing interest across the political spectrum in Washington in burdensharing.

Significantly, however, few responsible voices, either in America or Europe, argue that the end of the Cold War has eliminated the need for Western defense. All sides have shown some caution in considering possible changes in force structure, and the war in Chechnya is likely to reinforce this caution. But there has been a good deal of speculation about the roles which Western military units should play in the new situation, with the implication that force levels might be revised to match new functions.

Military analysis must start with an evaluation of potential security threats; it is only on this basis that it is possible to determine what forces are needed to provide an adequate defense. And this evaluation is particularly pertinent after the end of the Cold War: against what potential threats are Western forces now supposed to defend?

The answer here is twofold: the "classic" threat remains, though it is much reduced, and there is also a 'new,' threat. Each requires some thought and some adjustment in current thinking. And each is the subject of strategic and political debate on both sides of the Adantic.[21]

The "classic" threat is, of course, that posed by the residual strength of the Russian armed forces, with thousands of strategic nuclear warheads, a large nuclear-powered submarine fleet which continues to be modernized, the full range of advanced weaponry, and almost two million men under arms. At present, these forces are demoralized and their budget has been severely cut back. Over the last few years they have carried out a major withdrawal from Central and Eastern Europe, which has left their force structure in shambles. Their central purpose has been destroyed, and their country is going through a period of national confusion. The sad state of the Russian army has been exposed to the world by its inability to seize Grozny quickly and effectively.

But it would be a mistake to write off this military organization or its potential for threatening Western security. It is an organization with enormous pride and a demonstrated ability to survive the most challenging periods and come back strongly. It is actively looking for a new purpose, and appears to have found one in its ancient role—as the defender of the Russian nation. Its weight is felt very strongly in neighboring countries. In the coming years, its impact will depend heavily on the overall policies of the Russian government, the future of which is uncertain, to say the least.

The possibility that Russia might once again become a military threat to Western Europe is not discounted in Washington, although views on this possibility depend on one's perception of Russia's overall role. But Russian behavior in Chechnya and the near abroad, as well as its flirtations with Iran and Iraq, have tended to put planners in Washington on alert, and have encouraged caution in projecting any further force cuts in Europe. It would take time for Russia to once again become a military threat to Europe. Once Western forces are reduced, however, the Western democracies could take even longer to reassemble an adequate defense.

The "new" threat in Europe, as elsewhere, is the increased possibility of regionally destabilizing local conflicts, such as the current or recent wars in Croatia, Bosnia, Chechnya, Moldova, Georgia, and Nagorno-Karabakh. Western structures and military training have not focused on this type of threat, with the result that methods and techniques were inadequate when the conflict in Yugoslavia burst on the West. Both in the United States and in Europe there are now serious efforts to rectify this situation. The central problem, though, lies in identifying nascent conflicts and mustering the political will to intervene.

Local conflicts in Europe pose special questions for Washington. The Cold War rationale for the U.S. military presence was that a Soviet invasion would entail overwhelming military force which the Europeans could not match, and that they could only defend themselves if there were a large American contribution to their defense, including a link to the strategic nuclear deterrent. This rationale cannot be applied to local wars like Bosnia, because the conventional forces of Germany, France, Britain, Italy, and so forth could, in fact, secure Bosnia; and a nuclear threat is meaningless in small wars.

It is not the military capability which has been lacking in dealing with these local wars, but rather the political will. In such situations it is difficult to justify an American intervention. Washington's attitude toward Bosnia indicates that it does not consider its commitment to European security to extend automatically to such conflicts. For the first time it is evident that the NATO Treaty also limits the bases for U.S. involvement in European security problems.

This is not to say that the United States will never act in local wars in Europe, only that U.S. participation cannot be taken as a given. Americans cannot be expected to intervene in local European wars — much less those on the territory of the former Soviet Union — if the Europeans themselves cannot agree on how to respond to these conflicts. It seems clear that Washington will decide whether to participate in international interventions in local wars on the basis of the specific factors relevant to each conflict. And the final lesson of the Bosnian experience is that when the U.S. does not participate, it cannot lead.

NATO's Future

In view of the new political situation which has emerged, it may be desirable to acknowledge differing responsibilities for the two types of security problems that Europe now faces — the "classic" threat, and the "new" threat. Certainly a somewhat reduced NATO, with significant American involvement and the link to U.S. strategic forces; must remain intact to face the kind of threat for which it was created.

But for dealing with local conflicts like the one in Bosnia, the range of prevention, resolution, and reconciliation activities which are required should probably be the direct responsibility of the

Europeans themselves, either through the European Union and its security arm, the WEU, or through the OSCE. The United States may be involved in some of these activities, through its participation in the OSCE, or in specifically mandated NATO missions. But each such case will be subject to a specific political judgment and should not be taken to indicate the success or failure of America's overall commitment.

But the role of the 'international community must go beyond just responding to conflicts when they become violent. Fortunately, all the new states of the former USSR are members of the OSCE, along with the United States and the countries of the European Union. Thus the OSCE could be used in various constructive ways in this broad region. Indeed, it is the West's best vehicle for demonstrating concern for these new states, and for providing help in non-provocative ways. The OSCE has an excellent record of innovation in the field of preventive diplomacy and non-threatening intervention. Its low-key missions, with mandates tailored to the local circumstances, can be useful and are non-provocative. Such missions could be dispatched for visits or, in some cases, for longer periods, to help to monitor activities, understand problems, promote dialogue, or ease tensions. The OSCE's High Commissioner for National Minorities and its Office for Democratic Institutions and Human Rights (ODIHR) can also be helpful in these areas.

It would also be worthwhile to press Russia to agree to negotiate a basis on which it would accept Russian participation in peacekeeping or monitoring/observing Operations on the territory of the former USSR which were controlled or sponsored by the UN/OSCE. This will admittedly not be easy, since Russia holds that it has the right to carry out such operations either alone or under the guise of the CIS. Russia has to date refused all reasonable proposals to allow an international organization to control such a mission.

The challenge will be to demonstrate to the Russians, particularly the Russian military, that it is in their interest to share the burdens and responsibilities of these operations with the international community. The Russians do want their operations to be recognized as legitimate, and this offers some leverage to international negotiators. More fundamentally, Russia must be brought to understand that if it wishes to be accepted as a responsible member of the world community, it must play by the same rules as apply to other countries. President Boris Yeltsin has a direct responsibility for ensuring that Russia's military leaders, including Defense Minister Grachev; adhere to these rules.

The Western response to Russian policies has been ambiguous, largely because Russia's aims have themselves been unclear. But Russia's actions make it increasingly dear that Moscow is determined to regain control over all of the former USSR, with the possible exception of the Baltic states, and that its interventions in the near abroad are important tools for accomplishing this objective. The Chechen venture may signal a new willingness to use force, which could be repeated in the near abroad. Ultimately the West must decide what its attitude will be if and when Russia chooses to ignore established international standards and pursues its own interests on the territory of the former USSR beyond its own frontiers. Notably, the West will have to decide whether simply abandoning the new states of this region is compatible with its interests and principles.

In this situation NATOs central consultative role clearly remains valid and necessary. This continues to be the primary link between North America and Western Europe. Despite its utility for certain types of activity, the OSCE is not a substitute for this key relationship.

Through the North Atlantic Consultation Council (NACC), all the former member states of the Warsaw Pact, including all the new states of the former Soviet Union, are also present at NATO, and the Partnership for Peace has brought in many of the countries which were formally known as "neutrals." All of these countries will have something to say about the future shape of European security.

But the inner circle of this consultation process will continue to be that of the Alliance membership, and the likelihood is that these countries will want to preserve their collective defense arrangements for several years to come. In Washington, too, the consensus on this central point is likely to continue, regardless of differences over analyses and future roles. NATO is therefore sure to remain as the main element of the European security structure, at least for the immediate future.

The end of the Cold War is over, and it is time for a return to realism and prudence in planning for Western security.

Notes

1   "The Coming Anarchy," The Atlantic Monthly, February, 1994.

2   Russians like to use the term 'near abroad' for the newly independent countries around Russia's periphery. The term connotes a post-colonial paternalism, and is anathema to the states in this region, as well as other neighboring countries such as Finland and Turkey. Nonetheless it is a useful shorthand term and has gained currency.

3   Moscow News, December 16, 1992.

4   For another view of Russia's expanding efforts to regain control of the "near abroad," see Bruce D. Porter and Carol Saivetz, "The Once and Future Empire: Russia and the 'Near Abroad'," The Washington Quarterly, Summer; 1994.

5   See, for example, Therese Raphael, "Russia: The New Imperialism," The Wall Street Journal, June 22, 1994.

6   Strobe Talbott was a roommate of Clinton's when both were Rhodes Scholars at Oxford University. Talbott subsequently was a career journalist focused on the Soviet Union, and as Moscow bureau chief for Time wrote several cover stories on the USSR. He also distinguished himself as an author and expert on Soviet affairs, translating Khrushchev's memoirs and writing a best-selling account of U.S.-Soviet negotiations on nuclear weapons (Deadly Gambits). During a year as the State Department's Ambassador-at-Large for relations with the countries of the former Soviet Union Talbott shaped the Clinton administration's policy toward Russia. He was then promoted to the position of Deputy Secretary of State.

7   See, for example, Grachev's statement before a negotiating
    session on Nagorno-Karabakh that "Whatever I propose,
    that's what we're going to agree on," cited in Elizabeth Fuller,
    "The Karabakh Mediation Process; Grachev versus the
    CSCE?" RFE/RL Research Report, Vol. 3, No. 23, June 10,
    1994.

8   For background on the Nagorno-Karabakh dispute see "War
    in the Caucasus: A Proposal for Settlement of the Nagorno-
    Karabakh Conflict," Special Report, United States Institute of
    Peace, 1994.

9   When Presidents Clinton and Yeltsin met in Washington in
    September of 1994, the dispute over Russia's proposed
    "peacekeeping" role in the war over Nagorno-Karabakh was
    announced in advance by the White House as one of the key
    issues to be aired. Clinton did raise the problem, but the two
    could not agree on a formula for Russian participation in an
    international peacekeeping force, with Yeltsin insisting on
    Russian control of the operation. Prior to this meeting Clinton
    had met with both President Levon Ter-Petrossian of Armenia
    and President Gaidar Aliev of Azerbaijan, and had publicly
    committed himself to follow the Nagorno-Karabakh problem
    "personally." No sooner had Aliev signed a contract with a
    consortium of Western oil companies and asked for Clinton's
    support keeping Russian forces out of Azerbaijan than two of
    his close associates were assassinated in Baku.

10 For more than two years the CSCE has had an offer on the ta-
    ble to provide an international peacekeeping force to super-
    vise a ceasefire in the conflict over Nagorno-Karabakh, but
    this offer has been undercut by Russia's insistence on its own
    proposal for a Russian or CIS "peacekeeping" force. Although
    the Armenian side accepted the Russian proposal, Azerbaijan
    refused. A general agreement was reached on an OSCE force
    including Russians at the Budapest Summit of the OSCE on
    December 2-4, 1994, but important "details" such as the chain
    of command remained to be worked out.

11 See for example Henry Kissinger, "Expand NATO Now" in
    The Washington Post, December 19, 1994, and John J. Maresca,

"Russia's Gain is NATO's Loss," in Defence News, August 1-7, 1994.

12 On the Clinton administration's peacekeeping policy, see White House Press Release of May 5, 1994 concerning Presidential Decision Directive 25 on Reforming Multilateral Peace Operations also see, e.g., Elaine Sciolino, "New U.S. Peacekeeping Policy Deemphasizes Role of UN," in The New York Times, May 6, 1994, and Douglas Jehl, "U.S. Showing a New Caution on Peacekeeping Missions," in The New York Times, May 7, 1994.

13 For a more detailed analysis of Russia's post-colonial relationship with other states from the former USSR, see John J. Maresca, "Post-Independence Decolonization: A Framework for Analyzing Russia's Relations With Neighboring States" in James E. Goodby, ed., Regional Conflicts: The Challenge to U.S.-Russian Cooperation, SIPRI and the Oxford University Press, forthcoming, 1995.

14 See Raphael, op. cit.

15 Fora detailed analysis of the Russian approach to peacekeeping, in contrast to that of the West, see Pavel K. Baev, "Peacekeeping as a Challenge to European Borders," Security Dialogue, Volume 24 (2) pp 137-150.

16 Treaty on European Union, Title V, Article J.1.

17 Beginning in the spring of 1991, the Bush administration actively encouraged the European Union to take the leading role in dealing with the burgeoning Yugoslav crisis. At the meeting of CSCE Foreign ministers in Berlin, June 19-20, 1991, the United States negotiated a resolution on ending the Yugoslav confrontation, including gaining Yugoslav agreement to the text, and provided the fully agreed draft resolution to the representative of the EU so that it would be presented to the full conference as an EU initiative. The EU did indeed present it as their draft, and the resolution was approved by all the CSCE Foreign Ministers. This was the beginning of an uncertain and ultimately unsuccessful EU leadership role in responding to the disintegration of Yugoslavia.

18 See Baev, op. cit.

19 See John J. Maresca, "The War over Nagorno-Karabakh: The Agony of Indifference," in The Christian Science Monitor, Boston, 1994.

20 See, for example, Lally Weymouth, "Yalta" in The Washington Post, July 24, 1994, and Suzanne Crowe, "Breaking Russia's Peacekeeping Addiction," in The Wall Street Journal Europe, September 27, 1994.

21 For a more detailed analysis of Europe's current security problems, see John J. Maresca, "New Security Challenges in Europe," in Irish Studies in International Affairs, Volume 5, 1994, pp. 87-92, published by the Royal Irish Academy, Dublin.

Books and Articles published by
John Maresca, 1989-2024

1. "Strengthening Stability Through Openness," US Department of State, Washington, April, 1989

2. "To Helsinki — The Conference on Security and Cooperation in Europe, 1973-1975," Duke University Press, 1985, Second edition, 1987

3. "The End of the Cold War is Also Over," Center for International Security and Arms Control, Stanford University, 1995

4. "Russia's 'Near Abroad,' a Dilemma for the West," in "Crisis Management in the CIS; Whither Russia?" Nomos Verlag, Baden Baden, 1995

5. "The International Community and the Conflict Over Nagorno-Karabakh," in "Opportunities Missed, Opportunities Seized," Rowman & Littlefield, USA, 2000

6. "The CSCE At Its Inception: 1975 in Myth and Reality," in OSCE Yearbook, 2005, Baden-Baden, 2006

7. "Helsinki Revisited," ibidem-Verlag, Stuttgart, Germany, 2016

8. "The Unknown Peace Agreement," ibidem-Verlag, Stuttgart, Germany, 2022

9. "The Russian Operation," (novel) Edition Noema, ibidem, Stuttgart, Germany, 2022

10. "The Taliban in Texas," (novel) Edition Noema, ibidem, Stuttgart, Germany, 2023

11. "Ukraine: Putin's War for Russia's "Near Abroad," ibidem-Verlag, Stuttgart, Germany, 2024

Additional Reference Material

Helsinki Final Act:
https://www.osce.org/files/f/documents/5/c/39501.pdf

"Charter of Paris for a new Europe":
https://www.osce.org/files/f/documents/0/6/39516.pdf

"Helsinki" — Maresca paper from 1986.

"Agreement on Negotiations; the Inevitability of Compromise" — "To Helsinki," Duke University Press, Durham and London, 1985

"The People Have the Right to Choose" Herald Tribune, Paris, 1975

"Ensuring CSCE Promises are Kept," John Maresca, Bulletin of the OSCE (ODIHR), Warsaw, Fall, 1995

Official record of Maresca Congressional Testimony, Washington, 1993, published in "Helsinki Revisited," Ibidem, 2016

"Foreign Devils on the Silk Road — Take Two" John Maresca, China International Strategy Review, Beijing, China, 2015

"Countering Putin's Near Abroad Strategy," John Maresca, European Leadership Network, London, 2020